FEISTY AT FIFTY

Recently turned fifty herself, Sudha Menon, columnist, motivational speaker, writing coach, is the author of *Legacy: Letters from Eminent Parents to Their Daughters, Gifted: Inspiring Stories of People with Disabilities, Leading Ladies: Women Who Inspire India,* and more recently *Devi, Diva or She-Devil: The Smart Career Woman's Survival Guide.*

Advance Praise for *Feisty at Fifty*

'Well-known business journalist and author Sudha Menon has moved from the boardroom to the bedroom. *Feisty at Fifty* features her hallmark sharp, probing insights, but this time she goes under the covers. Witty, provocative and funny, sometimes achingly so' —Karen Anand, gourmand and food consultant

'Candid, fun, insightful ... an upbeat take on hitting the big five-oh' —Shobhaa Dé, author

'Wry and insightful, Sudha Menon pulls no punches in *Feisty at Fifty*. This is a glorious no-holds-barred journey of a woman in her fifties' — Kiran Manral, author

'A book all women and all men must read. Everyone will find something of their life in it'—Mahabanoo Mody-Kotwal, theatre artist

'Sudha has, with great poignancy, revealed the intense emotional bond between mother and daughter. Reading *Feisty at Fifty* invoked a strong sense of nostalgia in me and I found myself pining for my mother's loving, enveloping hug and for the wonderful treats she could rustle up in a jiffy. Oh, if only I could rewind the clock!' —Kalpana Morparia, CEO, South and Southeast Asia operations, J. P. Morgan Chase & Co.

'Sudha's book makes the dreaded fifties sound fabulous and fun. Touching and light-hearted, *Feisty at Fifty* is a breezy read with wise life lessons that stayed with me'—Leena Nair, Chief Human Resource Officer, Unilever

'I am no fifty-year-old woman, but a lot of the stuff Sudha writes about, including her insecurities and misadventures, resonated with me. As a comedian, I'm very critical of somebody else's humour but I found myself smiling and, sometimes laughing aloud, when I went through *Feisty at Fifty*'—Sundeep Rao, stand-up comedian and radio chat show host

Feisty at Fifty

HOW I STAY FABULOUS AT FIFTY-PLUS

SUDHA MENON

PAN

First published 2018 by Pan
an imprint of Pan Macmillan Publishing India Private Limited
707, Kailash Building
26, K.G. Marg, New Delhi – 110 001
www.panmacmillan.co.in

Pan Macmillan, 20 New Wharf Road, London N1 9RR
Basingstoke and Oxford
Associated companies throughout the world
www.panmacmillan.com

ISBN 978-93-86215-50-5

1 3 5 7 9 8 6 4 2

Typeset by R. Ajith Kumar
Printed and bound in India by
Replika Press Pvt. Ltd.

CONTENTS

TURNING FIFTY

SO HERE I AM, almost two years after I rushed headlong into my rendezvous with my fiftieth birthday, and I have survived to tell the tale. The truth is that the Big Five-oh is no big deal. For days you hold your breath in anticipation, tiptoe around the possibilities of the unknown, prepare yourself mentally and physically, but when it happens, it just does. The earth does not shift beneath your feet, the sky does not light up with streaks of lightning, and the temple bells certainly don't go off as they do in Bollywood movies. And when you wake up the next morning, you are still the same old you.

And yet, my fiftieth birthday was special in ways I cannot explain but can only appreciate. You know it is a special occasion when your spouse makes excuses galore to stay awake until the clock strikes midnight and then surprises you with a diamond ring to mark your fiftieth birthday. What made the ring more special for me is the knowledge that my forever shy and reserved spouse actually made the effort to walk into a jewellery showroom and ask a salesperson for a diamond ring for his wife. Coming from a man who hides behind the newspaper a whole lot, this was a great step.

'The idea of shopping was scary, so I went online and learnt a few things about diamonds before heading to the store. That way I could seal the deal in twenty minutes flat,' he told me sheepishly later that night as we lolled on the sofa eating chocolate and laughing about his great jewellery-buying adventure.

The morning of the birthday was special because I was treated to my favourite cup of ginger tea. As I sat with the newspaper, the spouse rustled up a cracking breakfast. Sounds mundane? Not if you have a routine where the spouse is out of the house first thing in the morning and you hit your work desk at 9 a.m. When you get to fifty, you appreciate the ordinary little things because you begin to realize that it is life's little moments that make for a happy, grand picture and a bag full of memories for your old age.

My fiftieth birthday was perfect in every way, beginning with a phone call from the kid sister and her darling husband encouraging me to splurge on some dresses that I had been dreaming about but never dared to buy. 'You only turn fifty once and this is our treat,' they chorused. I didn't need much persuasion after that.

Later that evening we drove down to Mumbai from Pune (where I live) and there I was showered with fresh surprises, small acts of kindness and thoughtfulness, all of which made my eyes well up. I walked into my sister's house, and Amma was waiting for me all giggly because her daughter had turned fifty, with a precious something to give me: her favourite gold necklace, the one she had spent years saving up to buy. Although she had hardly ever worn the necklace, she insisted that I should accept it. When I wore the necklace, it felt like being enveloped in Amma's warm hug. 'And when you have enjoyed wearing it, pass it on to your daughter, to remember me by,' she said. Any other time I would have laughed at her mushy talk, but Achan passing away six months earlier had put things in perspective for me: everything is transient, life is unpredictable, so cherish your loved ones when they are around.

The little niece had put up balloons and festoons everywhere and my daughter had baked the perfect cake to mark the day. There it was, a dazzling beauty, succulent with raspberry coulis, divine passion-fruit curd and almond sponge, all pulled together with sumptuous lashings of molten white chocolate. We are twin souls, the daughter and I, and believe in giving in to all things decadent when it comes to dessert.

Dinner that evening was special not just because there was a bottle of champagne and finger-licking kebabs, curries, and biryani, but also for the knowledge that I was surrounded by a family who loved me unconditionally, warts, moles, menopausal temper tantrums and all. I could not have asked for a better birthday gift than all the love that the universe showered on me that evening.

'So, how does it feel to be fifty?' a friend asked me the next day.

'Older, not necessarily wiser, but certainly happier,' I said to her. And never mind the jelly that was now jiggling on my belly from the unabashed revelry the day before.

Soon I will be approaching my sixties, but I am nowhere near done with life and having fun. I have things to do, places to visit, relationships to build – and some to heal; I have mountains to climb and a few scores to settle. Every year my bucket list grows longer, and even though I sometimes want to stop, being the frantic creature that I am, with my million to-do lists, I still want to visit Kashmir when it is at its resplendent best, see the Flamenco dancers in Spain and animals roaming wild in Africa. I want to do the salsa on a crowded dance floor without having my limbs freeze. And, when we can eventually manage to sync our crazy schedules, I want to go on a trip to Europe with Amma, my two sisters, my daughter and my niece, a trip where we dress up gorgeously, flirt with good-looking strangers, wander around admiring old churches and museums, and sit in street-side cafes eating cake and watching the world go by. I told you, I might be fifty, but the next fifty years of my life are going to be fabulous.

WHEN DAUGHTERS BECOME MOTHERS

ALL HELL BROKE LOOSE recently when a bitch gave birth to a litter of six in the children's play area of our gated community. The new mother had chosen to give birth right next to the children's swings, and half a dozen kids were either bitten or chased away by the snarling mommy who perceived them a threat to her own brood.

Every morning I watched her lick the pups clean and nuzzle them close to her as they suckled on her generous teats until falling asleep. She would shake them off gently to stretch herself, but not for a single moment would she take her eyes off the tiny souls she had brought into the world.

She did that for a few weeks, protecting her babies like a fierce tigress, inflicting encroachers with bites, the cure for which were painful anti-rabies injections. If only she could understand human language, she would have known the distress of the mothers of the kids who had suffered physical and emotional trauma from being attacked by an animal that had been their friend till she gave birth and turned into someone else.

The human mothers kept their children close to them, keeping them indoors and away from the snarling bitch, whose insecurity became worse as her tiny bundles started exploring the world around. Sitting on my balcony, sipping tea and watching the world go by, I could sometimes feel her anxiety as the little ones took their first steps away from her bosom to stare at a chirpy sparrow or a flitting butterfly, only to go rushing back when the sparrow chirped back a hello. Sometimes she would chase the sparrows away and at other times she would bring the errant offspring back into the fold.

Over the next few weeks I witnessed the miracle of nature as her anxiety gradually eased off, and one bright, sunny morning I observed the canine version of the rite of passage: as if in unison, her pack of six ventured out of the circle of her love and trundled out of the garden and into the real world. Mommy seemed sad yet relieved to see them disappear around the corner.

I see them occasionally now, mom and kids hanging around our housing complex, chasing after the occasional autorickshaw or neighbourhood cats, but it is now each to his/her own – none of the helicopter parenting we subject our offspring to, well into their adult life. Or, in my case, even when I have crossed the grand age of fifty.

I thought fifty would be a good time for Amma to stop telling me what to do and how to do it, but I don't have the nerve to stand up to her and set off an episode of her legendary sulking. Mother hen also has one hell of a temper; God save the one that sets it off!

Amma is the family's bearer of all kinds of news: pregnancies, elopements, marriages, and so on. Plus, truckloads of advice and life-saving exhortations. For instance, when the phone rang a little after midnight the other day, I picked it up to hear this: 'Aiyyyyooooyyoo… Your sister told me this morning you are off to Goa. Why do you want to go there? Don't you know my friend's sister's niece's son drowned in the sea there in 1995? Why can't you just be at home instead of roaming around all the time? The sea is dangerous.' And this from a woman who used to swim with abandon in the sea, coming as she does, from a village in coastal Kerala.

'Amma, it is past midnight. Can we talk about this tomorrow?'

'No! I can't sleep with the knowledge that you are going to Goa and taking your daughter along. Why do you have to expose her to the danger too? I have heard the place is full of Russian mafia who kidnap young girls…'

'Amma, that's enough now. I will take care of her. Now go to bed.'

Most mornings in the Menon household begin with a crisscross of telephone calls, some of them across continents because the matriarch does not believe in partiality and doles out advice to each female of her brood. My elder sister receives calls at 3 a.m. London time – Amma calling to tell her that she had made a great Malayali meal and had remembered her when everyone appreciated it. The matriarch is the proud owner of a smartphone which she knows not how to use, resulting in several people across the world regularly receiving video calls or half a dozen blank messages from her. Sometimes when the phone rings and it is her on the other side, she is actually bargaining with the vegetable vendor for a kilogram of raw mangoes. She has no clue that she has dumped a few kilos of veggies on her phone lying at the bottom of the shopping bag and that it has redialled the last dialled number. But I am digressing.

Some of my best conversations – and at times I have shown supreme restraint – are when she comes visiting from Mumbai, with a truckload of food to pamper Hassled Harry, who, she thinks, is deprived of love and food by her toughie daughter.

'You look tired,' she says, as soon as I stagger out of bed the next morning. 'You should sleep well. Sleep rejuvenates the mind and the body.'

'I would if you did not set off the pressure cooker at 4 a.m. to make sambar,' I think to myself. Amma has to cook first thing in the morning, no matter what. At my home she has the added incentive of feeding my forever-hungry spouse, who looks like he has been deliberately starved by his wicked witch of a wife.

'Also, you will sleep well if you do some meditation and yoga. I feel on top of the world these days,' she declares. Amma is very proud of her knowledge of meditation techniques, which she picked up from Buddhist monks at a temple near Wimbledon while visiting her elder daughter in London last year. She is hooked to the mindfulness meditation technique now and no conversation with her is complete without a lecture about it.

'You must practise walking meditation. When you are mindful and aware of every step you take, it takes your mind off unnecessary distractions and worries. It takes away all the stress and strain of your frantic life,' she says, unmindful of the fact that her 3 a.m. meditation practice has much to do with my stress this morning. And you would be stressed too, if the woman who gave birth to you took to waking up at 3 a.m. to meditate, make tea, and then do an hour of yoga before embarking on the mother-of-all cooking sessions.

Amma's conversations with me are freewheeling and don't stop at lectures on mindfulness. She is a frank woman, my mother is, and expresses herself freely on everything that concerns my life. Some mornings when I'm writing, she sidles up and plonks on the bed near my work desk, and I can feel one of her life lessons coming.

She: 'What are you writing?'

Me: 'My new book.'

She: 'What is it about?'

Me: 'About women.'

She: 'Time you changed your topic. You can't go on writing about women for the rest of your life. Try fiction now. Write a novel. You might make some money instead of being forever broke.'

Me (cringing): 'OK. Will try.'

She: 'What is there to try? Just do it. Don't be boring.'

Me: 'OK, Amma.'

But if you thought this is the end of the conversation, you are mistaken. Amma is nowhere near done yet.

She: 'Why do you want to write books? Why can't you get yourself a job? Look at your sisters, they have great jobs and good money. You should also study further.'

Me: 'Amma, I'm fifty-plus now. I don't want to find myself a job. I enjoy writing books and I hate the thought of going back to college.'

She: 'These are all excuses the timid adopt for themselves. And while we are on the topic, why did you allow that poor girl to become a chef? She is your only daughter. Do you want her to forever slog in the kitchen? Send her to Cambridge like your nephew. It will help her find a respectable career.'

Even when she's in Mumbai, Amma's conversations with me are endless and take place whenever she remembers to call me – anywhere from midnight to 3 a.m. or 2 p.m. These days she has started worrying about my fledgling's marital prospects and has been threatening to post her profile on a matrimonial site, with the result that I now have to ward off angry calls from the daughter.

Despite our occasional bickering I would have it no other way, though. I can't think of a world where the phone will ring and it will not be Amma on the other end, either guilt-tripping me about something or ticking me off about some omission or commission.

Speaking about mother-daughter exchanges, of late I have noticed, much to my own horror, that my conversations with my daughter bear a striking resemblance to Amma's phone calls with me. Every morning, at 9 a.m. sharp, the fledgling calls on her way to work. I wait to hear her voice, just like Amma waits to hear her brood's voices, and the fun begins within three minutes of her calling.

'Wot you doin'?' she asks, her voice smiling.

'Reading the newspaper,' I say.

'Good. What is happening in the world? I'm so busy I have not looked at a newspaper in ages...'

She shouldn't have said that. Not to a former journalist who lives and breathes the news even today. Besides, if she does not read the newspapers, how on earth is she going to know about the horrid things that are happening around the world?

'If you read the newspaper you would know that a young woman was attacked when she was travelling alone in the compartment of a Mumbai local train at 11p.m. I keep telling you to please avoid travelling alone very late. Get into a general compartment if need be. Also, the newspaper said the man accosted her to get her mobile phone. If she was not so engrossed in her phone, she would have noticed that a guy was getting into her compartment and she could have raised an alarm or got off at the station as soon as he boarded. I always tell you to not lose yourself in your phone while travelling. Be aware of your surroundings.'

'Yes, Mom.'

'And what about your lunchbox? Have you tossed the plastic one and bought a steel one instead? Plastic leaks paraben and is carcinogenic. Also, have you started putting the phone away from your head when you go to bed? That could also make you sick. And what about telling your business partner that you need more time for yourself and can't slog round the clock? Your business is not your entire life. Learn to be assertive when you talk, and no one will exploit you.'

'Mom, I love you very much, but this is me being assertive: stop advising me first thing every day. I'm twenty-six, not six! I can take care of myself. Now go back to your laptop and write your book. Love you.'

I must confess that I never thought I would become my mother. But I have. I realized it the other day, just after the fledgling told me off about constantly lecturing her, that I now do all the things that I promised myself I would never do. I stayed silent for forty-eight hours after being ticked off but was back on the phone doling out instructions about taking her vitamins on time, being prudent with money, and, most important, her love life. When it comes to parenting, whoever talked about Tiger Mom has not met me; when it comes to my daughter's love life, I have reserved the right to tell her a lot of stuff and then some. Boys who drink, smoke and party too much won't do. Nor will boys who don't remember her birthday, are discourteous, slovenly and ill-groomed. The boy she dates must be well-read, a star in the kitchen, must love old Hindi film songs, and, above all, must fit into the family headed by the grand matriarch, her brood of three daughters – who are mother hens personified – and a clutch of uncles and cousins.

The other day somebody told me about a girl who was so much in love with her boyfriend that she spent her entire day hanging around, catering to his every whim and fancy. In the end the guy told her she was too clingy and dumped her unceremoniously. My heart went out to the young girl who had effaced herself under some mistaken notion of love and courtship. I was on the phone a minute after I heard this story. 'Make sure you are never, ever in a relationship with a guy who orders you around. Make sure you are not available for any man who makes you do as he pleases at the snap of his fingers. Cultivate your own interests and make sure those interests get as much time as your boyfriend does.'

'Yes, Mom,' the fledgling replied. 'If there is any man left in the country who fits your bill and the specifications of your sisters, I will make sure that I am not always available to him,' she teased.

As I disconnected the phone I suddenly remembered a conversation I had with Achan long ago, about my daughter and my constant concern about her well-being. 'You have given her good education and a solid set of values. Now leave her to make her choices, make mistakes and learn from those mistakes. We all learn from the bruises that we get along the way. Such is life,' he had told me. I am going to try very hard to follow his advice.

BONDING OVER FOOD WITH AMMA

LAST YEAR, FOR THE first time in almost thirty years since I married against my parents' wishes and moved out of my childhood home, I spent an entire month with Amma. Much water has flown under the bridge since the twenty-one-year-old me went off with a young man Amma initially disapproved of but eventually came to love. This time the roles were reversed, and it was me doing the mothering and she being the rebellious, quick-tempered, irreverent child that I used to be.

Those were a testing four weeks for both of us. She tested my patience and I failed miserably. Patience and I are strangers. The few people who love me have waited for me to develop patience but have since given up. The four weeks that I spent 'mom-sitting' Amma in my sister's townhouse near London – while she was travelling for work – turned out to be part Bigg Boss and part two adults playing house. And just so you know, Big Mama was the bully and I, the victim. She drove me mad with her mulishness, her complete disregard for rules that I set around the house, and her insistence that we had to gad about town every moment of the day because 'we only live once'.

Only, her idea of living involved stopping every half an hour to eat fries, scones and clotted cream or pink-and-yellow cupcakes wherever she saw a patisserie. Considering that she is a diabetic and I had been cautioned by elder sis to make sure she ate plenty of healthy food, this was a complete no-no; but then who was to bell *this* cat? One morning I woke up and couldn't find Amma in her room. I panicked momentarily but that was before I saw the larder open and simply followed the trail of cake crumbs to the garden swing where she sat happily polishing away a giant fruit cake. 'Diabetes has nothing to do with food. It is to do with stress. You make sure you don't stress me,' she said, in between slurping ginger tea from a large mug and biting into a thick slice of cake.

I used to believe I was a smart cookie who effortlessly came up with original excuses to avoid homework as a kid. But that was before I saw Amma in action last summer. I would jump out of bed every morning, brush, get into my track pants, and walk into the matriarch's room, and there she would be, curled into a ball under the duvet, only her woebegone face visible. 'I have some pain in my leg. My arthritis is acting up,' she would whisper; if a casting director were around, Amma would promptly have landed herself any number of roles as a mother in Bollywood films.

Our walks came to be dictated by Amma's weather predictions, BBC Weather be damned. 'It is too grey and dreary, and I don't want to walk today,' she would declare, settling herself down on the plump sofa from where she got up only at lunchtime. Another day it would be,'It is too bright today. The sun is closer to the earth in this part of the world and we might get sunburnt,' wagging her finger to push home the point. One morning it would be a rumble in her heart, another day a buzz in her head.

The only thing that would ever get her out of the bed or off the couch was the prospect of our 4 p.m. walk to High Street. For me it was a great way to tone my body and shed some weight, but Amma, clearly, had not heard about the joy of being in the journey and not in hankering after the destination. Her destination was the bearded lady who held court all day from her food truck in the town square, conjuring up golden, crispy fries, sumptuous burgers, and weak, watery tea, in between subjecting everybody to a healthy dose of local goss. If it was not the food truck, Amma would head to Gregg's, where she would stand gazing at rows upon rows of colourful, infinitely enticing pastries, cupcakes, apple and cinnamon buns, and her favourite scones and clotted cream.

Ever tried dissuading a kid from putting her hands into a candy jar? Dissuading Amma was the same: every evening I would try everything to keep her away from the sugary treats – and every time she would con me into parting with a few pounds to buy herself a treat. 'When you travel to a foreign country you have to eat their food and live like them,' she pronounced one day, sinking her teeth into a gorgeous chocolate pastry, while I clenched my fist to prevent myself from grabbing it and taking a tiny bite. 'Besides, we only live once. What is the use of money if it can't buy you happiness?' she said, licking gooey chocolate cream off her fingers.

By the time we reach the age of fifty most of us have notched up plenty of regrets and I-wish-I-had moments to last a lifetime. While I have a large collection of these, the single biggest regret I nurse is that I allowed marriage and life to distance me from the two people who loved me the most. Achan passed away a couple of years ago, without me ever telling him what it meant to have him in my world. He was the man who defined me, the fiercely protective papa bear who believed his scrawny, mousy, forever-rebellious second-born was the most beautiful girl in the world. He gave me the wings to fly but then I flew so far away that I never made it back to his nest to tell him that even though his fledgling had discovered the world, he meant the world to her. Between setting up my own home, managing a demanding career and motherhood, and everything that comes along with it, including play dates, birthday parties, and PTAs, the years went away in such a blur that I never noticed when Amma and Achan went from being an energetic, busy couple to a twosome who waited for the doorbell to ring and for one of their brood to come calling. Amma, especially, took it badly. She never could come to terms with the fact that her once-bustling home was now empty with nobody to keep her company but the silent walls that reverberated with the memories of her grandchildren's happy laughter.

Last summer Amma and I found each other again. It was strange at first to wake up in a house where it was just us. Sometimes the silence hung heavy in the air, pregnant with unspoken thoughts and unanswered questions. And like strangers at airport lounges or on long-distance flights, we put on our best faces and pussyfooted around each other, unwilling to allow the fragile connection that we were forging to snap.

It took a few days of hard work, but the awkwardness soon fell away and, miraculously, one day we were mother and daughter once again. I knew that for sure when I walked into the kitchen and found her busy as a bee, chopping, sautéing, frying and steaming like her life depended on it. I objected, saying I had work to do and could not spare time for cooking elaborate meals, and she said to me: 'You go do your work. Don't bother yourself with this stuff. All I have ever done with my life is cook for my children, and even though you might think it a nuisance, this is what I love to do. Lunch will be ready at 1.'

At lunch that day I became the little girl I used to be who rushed home after school to polish off a large plate piled high with a mound of rice, at the centre of which she made a hole to pour a river of drumstick sambar. Amma had remembered that I liked to crush a couple of pappadams into the sambar and had fried up a dozen. I ate like I had not eaten in a long time, smacking my lips and wiping off the last drop of sambar from my plate, leaving Amma glowing with happiness and pride about the unfailing ability of her food to keep her brood close to her.

I will never forget how Achan, who had slipped into a semi-conscious state during the days before his passing, miraculously regained consciousness one morning and asked Amma to make him her signature stew and idlis. When we were kids, Amma would complain that her hands were about to fall off from making endless rounds of idlis and stew. I don't think Amma realized that morning that it would be Achan's last meal, but in retrospect she is happy that she cooked it quickly and fed him patiently, one slow bite after the other, till he was happy and full.

Back in London, Amma would inevitably follow up her last morsel from lunch with,'What do you want to eat tomorrow?' and I would bite back my impatient response and name one of my old favourites. Amma's mood, sombre most of the summer, lifted dramatically as we rediscovered each other over memorable meals seated at my sister's round rosewood table, Yesudas crooning in the background.

When I look back, last summer was as much about Amma's discovery of herself through the legacy she had built for her family: some days the tangy, vibrantly coloured avial became tangier with her anecdotes about how Onam and Vishu, the two big festivals for us Malayalis, was celebrated back in the days she was a child in our ancestral home in Kerala. Our sprawling home was the anchor around which half a dozen families who worked on our farm lived and the week-long celebrations included all of them. Amma's eldest aunt, a formidable single woman, was the matriarch who got everybody together a week before the festival, handing out responsibilities to each one of them. The menfolk had to go about the job of procuring the best ingredients for the sadhya – great bunches of raw plantains, plump red and yellow pumpkins, drumsticks, tender yam, dozens of coconuts, jaggery, sacks full of rice and dal, great amounts of pearl onions.

The back of the house, where the kitchen was located, would be the epicentre of all activity, especially on festival days. The women who helped around the house would arrive early, fresh from a dip in the temple pond, long hair still dripping water, and get to work for the lunch, grating dozens of coconuts, chopping large amounts of vegetables, and setting the milk to boil in large *uruli*s that could hold enough payasam to feed fifty people. Amma reminisced about hanging around the women as they pounded and ground the spices for the ten to twelve different curries for the sadhya menu; while the bright yellow avial would require roughly ground coconut, green chilli and cumin seeds, the sambar required a combination of roasted whole coriander, whole red chillies, fenugreek seeds, curry leaves and grated coconut that had been toasted till it attained the right shade of pink, all ground to a smooth, silken consistency.

Then there was the entire ritual of making the coconut milk that went into the payasam and some curries. First, a couple of women sat in the kitchen veranda, grating the coconut and squeezing out the milk that would go into a curry and payasam. The second stage involved sprinkling a bit of water to the squeezed, grated coconut to coax out the remaining milk that would mingle with the curries to give it a smooth consistency. The women handling the coconut milk were delegated exclusively the task of preparing the payasam on a wood-fired stove placed away from the bubbling pots of fiery sambar, sour *injipuli*, avial, and other curries, which if they found their way into the *paalpradaman*, would cause the milk to curdle instantly.

The avial, a medley of summer vegetables cooked in a coconut-and-yogurt gravy, was always made in large quantities during Onam, and seated at the table in faraway London, Amma giggled over her memory of how the children squabbled for the last spoonful of avial in the pan, on the third day of Onam by when it would have fermented and be the tastiest. 'Even the family cows, Rambha and Rama, had a great time during festivals because they got to eat ripe plantains by the dozen and all the leftovers from the kitchen.'

Another day Amma would reminisce about the way her unmarried aunts ran the kitchen. No unexpected guest, even if they turned up after the family had finished lunch, went away unfed. 'Nobody cursed the guest or grumbled about the hard work. All it took was for one of the ladies to go pluck tender moringa leaves from the tree that grew behind the kitchen and sauté them into a light *thoran* with fresh shavings of coconut. Another member of the kitchen staff would, in the meantime, pick a couple of raw mangoes, chop an onion, grab a couple of red chillies to roast in the wood-fired stove, and grind a spicy, tart mango chutney that was the perfect accompaniment for the meal, along with pappadam.There would always be some fresh bananas from the backyard or *unni appams*, sweetened with jaggery and soft-centred with the bananas that had gone into the batter before they were fried.'

Amma can talk about food endlessly. Some days it irritated me – I wonder now if that was because it showed me as the reluctant queen of my own kitchen – and I would snap at her. The shine would disappear from her eyes, peering at me from behind glasses smudged with oil and turmeric stains, and she would retreat into the kitchen to seek comfort in the old, familiar things, cooking another pot of comforting rice and curry. It would wrench my heart to see her then, her shoulder slumped from the unexpected rejection of the only way she knows to show great love for her children, and I would make amends at lunch by eating much more than I really wanted to and all would be well again.

'Your father loved this potato fry very much,' she recalled one day as she stood at the kitchen stove, frying a mixture of ground onions and fiery red chillies into which she added chopped, boiled potatoes. 'You must learn how to make it because your daughter and he would compete for the last piece of potato in the pan when she used to live with us,' she said, and there it was, yet another way of bonding with my Amma. 'I would love to learn cooking from you. Will you teach me?' I asked, and she looked at me unbelievingly because I was the only one of her three daughters who had refused to enter the kitchen while growing up.

'Someday, when you have your own children, you will know the value of what I am saying,' she would caution me and I would toss my hair and look at her with disdain and reply, 'When I have children, I will have a cook who will feed them whatever they want to eat. Not just boring sambar and idlis.' Almost four decades later I know today that no matter how many fancy meals she eats, my twenty-six-year-old daughter, a pastry chef, looks forward to the comfort of eating a plateful of steaming hot dal khichdi that I prepare for her when she visits. It is not just the ghee and the pappadam that add zing to the simple meal; I know it is the endless love that passes from me to her when I prepare it.

Our summer together took on a rhythm and ritual of its own with Amma cooking breakfast and lunch, and napping until our 4 p.m. walk, when she would dress up in trousers and a cardigan, and, just when we would be all set to step out, she would declare that she had forgotten to wear her compression socks. She would disappear into the bedroom and the trousers would come off and she would begin the circus of pulling up the compression socks, struggling to get them up to the thighs, the exercise tiring her so much that she would collapse onto the bed, panting. Nobody in the family is clear which doctor prescribed the compression socks for Amma and for what period she was to wear them, but Amma declares, dramatically, that if she were to not wear them, her varicose veins would burst and spout blood and she would die on the spot. Only the very foolish or the extremely brave in the family will question Amma on her thorough knowledge of varicose veins, compression socks, heart ailments, arthritis, and such other. She insists she suffers from all these and that the only reason she is alive are the eighteen pills she swallows post meals every day!

The trick, for me, was to make sure that I caught her every afternoon at the right moment, just before she put on her trousers and stand there till she pulled on the socks and then the trousers, in that order. Time and the passage of time mean nothing to Amma. She once missed a flight to Kerala because she went into the airport loo, and my poor husband, who was accompanying her, could do nothing about it but anxiously hang around outside, wishing she would come out. He called her endlessly but, of course, her phone did not have charge. When she eventually emerged and they rushed to the boarding gate, the aircraft was already cruising for take-off. Amma was not in the least perturbed. She said she was pinning up her saree pallu because it was not pinned properly. 'It is only a flight. We can take another one,' she told me when I called her up in a flap to scold her. In another version of the same story, Amma insisted it was my husband who had taken too long in the loo and caused them to miss the flight.

With each passing day, with every walk through shaded alleys and parks bursting with summer blooms and berries, we became mother and daughter once again, with nobody else to fill the gaps in the conversation. We were careful to not upset the fragile bond that we were reconstructing; it was a strange sort of coming together, tentative at first because we were both unsure of how this would go.

Walking along pathways and apple trees heavy with fruit, she would become a child all over again, gathering the fruit from the ground and spiriting it away into her favourite cloth bag. Some days her shirt front would be all red and blue from the blackberries, blueberries, and raspberries that she plucked off the shrubs and popped into her mouth, the juice trickling down her chin. Amma has her rules about eating fruits and berries that she finds: anything fallen on the ground must be taken home and washed because it is sure to have dog or cat poo or pee on it. Berries plucked from the shrubs are safe for instant consumption.

Some days she would be sombre, her shoulders sagging from the weight of some unspoken grief, and one day it came out when I scolded her for her lack of spirit. 'Last summer your father and I walked along this road and he plucked berries for me from these shrubs. I never imagined he would go away so soon. We were supposed to visit Scotland together this year and he was looking forward to it,' she said, her eyes misting with the memory of her companion of fifty-three years.

When Achan passed away two years ago, she was devastated and plunged into a depressive state, retreating into herself and shutting all of us out. She raged and ranted against her god, accusing him of treating her unjustly even though she served him with devotion. She turned on us with a rage that we never thought she was capable of and drove us to tears of frustration with her accusations of negligence. The trip to London, where my elder sister lives, was part of our plan of action to distract her and take her away from the Mumbai home where memories of Achan haunted her.

Back home from our walk, Amma would sit on the garden swing, singing to herself and reading. She was full of wonderment that it could be 8 p.m. and still be bright as day. Dinner was my time to treat her and she would watch fascinated as I chopped mushrooms, sautéed them in butter, and made a mushroom cappuccino to go with rosemary potatoes that I made with herbs freshly plucked from the garden. I never thought a day would come when I would hear Amma appreciate my cooking, and my heart filled with pride one evening when she bit into my take on a quesadilla, bursting with the flavours of grilled asparagus, red and yellow peppers, homemade sour cream, and guacamole. 'In our times we just ate food that our mothers cooked and never learnt any other cuisine because we never travelled anywhere.' Sitting in the garden one evening and enjoying her evening meal – I had rustled up roasted tomato and garlic soup, with garlic toast and grilled mushrooms on the side – Amma swore that she was in love with my ability to make a different soup every day.

'Will you teach me how to make this? It is the best thing I have eaten in a long time,' she declared.

That evening we started our joint project: she would talk to me about the food that she grew up with and I would tell her about the food that I learnt to cook during my travels. Amma struggled to recollect recipes of family favourites, went off on tangents and narrated anecdotes and family lore around particular dishes, laughed aloud over memories of cooking gone awry, and shed a tear or two when she remembered loved ones who had given her the priceless legacy of their great love for food. Amma's method of narrating recipes – 'a pinch of turmeric, a handful of coriander seeds, a little fenugreek, and some grated coconut' – would often drive me crazy because I am a complete measurements and follow-the-recipe-book kind of person.

As I took down the recipes, my mind was busy capturing those moments with my mother, filing the precious moments of our togetherness in the back shelf of my mind to cherish forever.

I may or may not prepare the dishes that she so lovingly gave me the recipes for, but what I got from her was a learning that is far more precious. The four weeks with her in a distant land taught me all about unconditional love, the value of tirelessly devoting oneself to the people we love. Seeing her in action taught me about resilience, persistence, the refusal to let anything and anybody pull you down. From her fierce loyalty and her boundless admiration of her children, I learnt to trust and have faith in myself and my own. My relationship with my daughter often runs into rough weather because I am wont to question what I see as her timid and pliable nature. Being with Amma taught me the virtue of letting my child be just who she is and trust that she knows what is best for her.

My most rewarding moment that summer with my mother came unexpectedly. Amma and I were enjoying a thin-crust pizza, fragrant with rosemary, homemade sauce, veggies and burnt garlic, when my sister called from India. 'You know, our Sudha has finally grown up.

She is a good cook now. Her grandchildren will be well fed. Achan would have loved this pizza she has made for us,' she gushed into the phone. I had finally passed muster with Amma and that meant way more to me than any of my other achievements. Somehow, I am sure my dear, departed father would be pleased.

FEAR OF FLYING

THERE ARE TRAVELLERS AND more travellers and then there is me. The night before I have to fly, I have a bad case of the jitters. I toss and turn in bed, wander around in the middle of the night to ensure I have carried my identity proof, a printout of the ticket, and enough money (yes, I belong to the old world), then get back into bed and toss for another couple of hours and jump out of bed at 3:30 a.m. sharp for my 6 a.m. flight.

By the time I am ready to leave, I am exhausted and want to get right back into bed. Hassled Harry has wisely learnt to keep his counsel to himself and snores gently on a chair as he waits for me to finish my final round of rummaging in my bag for things lost and found. I suspect when he finally drops me off at the airport he lurks around to make sure I have checked in, and then does a celebratory jig to welcome blissful solitude of a few days.

I don't know what I hate more about the time I spend waiting around in airports. In the beginning it used to be the waiting in serpentine queues for check-in, begging for aisle seats, and other forms of grovelling that ordinary mortals flying Shashi Tharoor's famed 'cattle class' are forced to do. A friend of mine once told me she arrives very late for her flights and, because she is very fashionably turned out, the staff routinely upgrade her. I have never mustered the courage to do that. Besides, the way I dress while I travel, I am more likely to be arrested on charges of suspicious behaviour than be upgraded. Thanks to relentless travel I have almost got used to cringe-inducing experiences such as the occasional feel-up by the female security. Maybe it is just me, but I think they can do better at security than sadistically poking you in the breast with the metal detector.

By the time I have cleared security and arrived in the magical land of the departure area, my hair is dishevelled, my clothes are in disarray with the dupatta trailing after me like Kate Middleton's wedding gown, and my eyes are darting around wildly in search of a place to rest my butt and get the heavy bag off my shoulder. I have seen fellow travellers sneak suspicious looks at me from the corner of their eyes as I frantically search for something or the other in my bag. I am a chronic searcher of things at airports – I misplace the boarding pass at least half a dozen times and then find it right under my nose. The rest of the time I am searching for my phone, which also disappears into the big black hole that is my bag.

It is usually when I am the most hassled and dishevelled that I run into some of the glamorous people I know and who, sadly, also know me. Just the other day I was sitting on yet another plastic chair in some big city airport, looking wistfully at this glam woman pacing up and down in a canary yellow jacket, fashionably retro skirt, and knee-high boots, talking animatedly on the phone, her silken hair cascading down her back. I was eating my own heart out in envy and throwing mental darts at her shapely, unsuspecting backside when she turned, and our eyes met, and she turned out to be this television anchor who has most of the nation – or at least one half of the nation – eating out of her hand, thanks to her blinding beauty. 'Oh, how are you?' she asked, giving me the once-over, obviously curious to know why I looked like I had run away from a mental asylum. 'I am fine,' I replied weakly, trying to hide my well-used Skechers-clad feet under the chair and kicking myself for having worn my ancient, comfortable baggy jeans and a baggier T-shirt for the flight. I would love to be one of those gorgeous beings that arrive at the airport with freshly blow-dried hair, impeccable make-up, fabulous clothes, and 'it' bags. These fashionable people head to equally fashionable airport cafes or bars where they hang out, picking at tiny morsels of expensive food, while basking in the admiring glances of those around them.

I have developed other conditions that attack me while I wait in the queue to board the flight. First off is the great wave of envy that engulfs me when those with business and first-class tickets get to toss their hair and sweep past mere mortals waiting in queue to board. They have the staff bowing and scraping before them, while all I get is a nasty kid in his mom's arms, kicking at my backside with a viciousness you would reserve for adults. But I also envy mothers with babies in their arms because they too get to board while we still wait in the queue. Possibly the only time I will envy this segment, though, because I know what lies in store for them. Raising kids is not what it used to be in the olden times and I have great admiration for those who have knowingly set out on that journey.

Getting on board is only a fraction of the job done, though. When you board a flight these days there are all kinds of dangers to life and limb, such as slobs carrying backpack weaponry who hit you on the face as they turn this way and that while looking for their seat, clueless that they socked you on the jaw multiple times; or, you might be in danger from the folks who are steering the aircraft and taking you from point A to B. I read the other day how the pilot and co-pilot of a long-haul flight had got into a fight and come to blows, and in the ensuing chaos left the controls unattended. Now, I have nothing against a good fight, but I do think the pilots could have chosen the timing and location of their fight a bit sensibly. I haven't stepped into a flight in the last few months without praying hard for myself and my fellow passengers. But more than that I pray for the two people in the cockpit. 'Dear God, let there be love in abundance between the two pilots' is the prayer I send up just as soon as the flight takes off. And I mean love of the brother–sister kind, not the other. The other type could be distracting to say the least and it is best left alone thousands of feet up in the air.

Meanwhile, coming back to more mundane things like hunger. Ever tried to eat an in-flight paneer tikka or paneer paratha? You might as well eat your Kolhapuri chappal! But wait, considering that we are no longer allowed to do away with cows, there might soon be no Kolhapuri chappals to eat either. Keeping the mouth zippered is a great way to shed some weight and I am practising it to great effect. That better than having to eat biryani, noodles or a make-it-yourself upma in the sky. For breakfast. No jokes. This is exactly what I find on board these days on morning flights. I wish I could introduce Amma to the people who plan breakfast menus for airlines. Amma is a south Indian breakfast snob who believes that there is no ailment or problem that a good helping of idlis and dosas cannot heal or solve. If you were to put her in charge of an airline menu, passengers would be less cranky and quarrelsome because they would all be snoozing after having a bellyful of velvety idlis, chutney, sambar, mulagapodi (or gunpowder as it is also known), crisp dosas, and soft uttappams.

The only problem for me in such a situation is that there would be too many men who would fall asleep and use your shoulders as headrests. And as if that is not bad enough, what do you do with folks whose musical snores fill up the cabin?

THERE'S A CHILL IN MY BEDROOM

OF LATE, THERE HAS been a chill in the bedroom. And I am not talking about the old, cranky air conditioner that works with deadly efficiency in peak winter and moans and groans when it has to perform in the summer. I am talking about Hassled Harry, moi, and the decided lack of any heat between the sheets. The only moans and shudders in our bedroom are that of the ACs. And when the two occupants of the room moan and shudder, it is largely because of arthritic joints or a touch of indigestion. Sigh!

Come bedtime and our man slinks into bed – after thirty minutes of watching Arnab Goswami steamroll everyone in sight – and slides to his side of the bed till sleep overcomes him and the bedroom trembles with his reversing-the-tractor snoring act.

I don't know what has been annoying me more, the snoring or the sustained lack of chemistry – or, physics – in the bedroom. Occasionally, I do feel like the woman scorned, but I am not sure I want to take the trouble or even keep awake enough to seduce the old man. I did try the age-old female tactics – some deep sighing, lots of tossing and turning about in bed, and, once, switching on the light and making a show about swallowing a Crocin. If I thought I would get attention, any sort of attention, I was mistaken. My spouse – God bless his snoring soul – has the ability to sleep through a tsunami, so my theatrics were not about to wake him up.

After months of worrying about the lack of action in my life I have come to realize a few things, the first and the most important being that I don't really miss it. There, I said it. I think the twenties and thirties are when we have our best sex. We can do it anywhere and any number of times and still want more. In your early forties you savour it a bit more because it gets a little difficult for the body to keep pace with the desire. In your late forties you cling to the libido like a drowning man would clutch at a straw, because you know that you are probably soon going to say goodbye to the one thing that made the marriage exciting. By the time you are fifty the libido gives a last dying gasp. When guys of fifty say they scored big time, it probably means they managed to have sex once that month. These days I have begun to take men who talk big (ahem) about their exploits in bed with more than a pinch of salt.

Most men I know would be outraged by this joke I am about to share with you but heck, who cares? You know what they say about men and their cars: the smaller the P, the bigger the car!

But I am digressing here. We are on the topic of sex and the middle-aged couple and I am not sure it is even a relevant subject because I think by the time you and the grumpy half have been married thirty years, there is too much familiarity to breed any sex. Your breeding has been done by then and that brood is always around reminding you of your advancing age. Some of that brood have dumped their brood on you so they can go get themselves a life, so all you do with the old man is hold hands in bed and dream your separate dreams. There was a time I would dream of steamy sex, but these days I mostly fantasize about gulab jamuns and crisp toast dripping with butter.

I think there is an epidemic of 'sexlessness' (my term, you won't find it in the dictionary) among the middle-aged in this country but most of these pot-bellied men or powerful honchos who are too overworked to get it up would rather die in a ditch than admit it. Don't believe me? Go read the agony columns in newspapers where countless middle-aged men pour their tormented hearts out to a stranger, all in the hope that he will have some magic potion that will get them up and about like Energizer bunnies.

If you read these columns you will find that when they cross the Big F (fifty, before you start imagining it's the other F word) many men are so completely obsessed with the size that their self-esteem depends on it: it measures five inches when erect, is that good, sir? Or is it too small to satisfy my wife?

Some of them sweat over its shape: My P is curved and when erect, it bends to the right.

Others are frantic about their plummetting abilities: I used to have sex seven days a week. Now, I can hardly do it once every six months. Is there something I can do to enjoy sex like I used to?

Depending on how much action Agony Uncle/Aunt has been getting in their own lives, their answers are telling, scorching, or completely hilarious.

Dear Uncle, if your five inches have satisfied your wife until now, no reason it won't later.

Or, Dear five-inches-small, this is a question you should have asked your wife twenty-five years ago!

Or, Dear Horny Rabbit, I am dying of envy. Till what age did you have sex seven times a week? You dirty dog, you can't have all the good luck in the world. There is no way in hell you can have sex that many times anymore.

Various men have devised various ways to shore up or revive their dead libido. Some find nubile nymphets to get their rocks off, some watch porn, some buy bigger cars, and yet others use their pillows or other handy items which don't require them to put in any extra effort. And women go shop and hang out with their friends.

Be that as it may, the chill factor in our bedroom has not had the least effect on our marriage. If anything, it has improved our relationship. We are now almost siblings and love each other unconditionally, just as siblings do. Now we don't feel the pressure of having to perform, no need to make a pretence of how much we love the steaming action in bed and how much we look forward to hitting the sack. In fact, we are so friend-zoned that we actually slouch on the sofa watching telly post dinner and have a good laugh about the lack of sex in our lives.

The other day, though, during a casual lunch with the girls, one of them blurted out that her sex life was dead and gone. There was a moment of stunned silence and then the air was thick with tips and suggestions and, strangely enough, most of them had to do with sexy lingerie. 'If you are going to wear mommy underwear chances are you'll be treated like a mommy. Go get yourself some lingerie that screams "I'm available" and watch the old man heat up the action,' one from the gang said.

Her words set me thinking. I have spent the last ten years of my life wearing bras in black, white and nude. Same as my panties. I buy mine in five minutes flat at the neighbourhood mall and head off to the shoe store. So what if my sex life is insipid and colourless? I have shoes in every colour of the rainbow. Beats the hell out of sex, believe me. And lasts way longer!

A NOT-SO-UPLIFTING STORY

I MISS THE GOOD old days when a bra was a bra was a bra and you just started wearing one because your mother told you it was time to wear one. I remember how excited I was when Amma told me it was time I started wearing a bra. It had been months since my classmates, many of them plump and well-rounded, had started showing off their bra lines, leaving me feeling decidedly less endowed, in more ways than one.

To my teenaged mind and to the painfully scrawny body that I possessed in those days, wearing the bra would have saved me from the life of a wallflower. Nothing is worse for a teenaged soul than having siblings who are gorgeous and enjoy the undying loyalty of all the neighbourhood boys. Add this to the knowledge that there isn't the faintest sign of your own blossoming into a woman with breasts, and the battle is lost even before it begins.

I remember my lack of boobs being a matter of much mirth among the family matriarchs. I had a grandmother plus three unmarried grand-aunts, all of them generously blessed in the assets category under discussion. During sultry summers, when we visited the ancestral home in Kerala, the matrons would embark on a mission to plump me up, so that I would begin resembling a woman. I don't know about the rest of the country, but in Kerala in those days it was perfectly acceptable for the neighbourhood women or even folks who lived on the other side of the village to drop in for tea and fried banana fritters and idly chat about this and that. Only, in this case, the this-and-that largely involved my appearance.

'Why is she so thin?' one matron, my grandma's old classmate, would begin, and the rest of the gang would quickly pounce on the subject of the flatness of my chest. 'Someone can play tennis on her chest,' another old hag would cackle, and all the while I would sit there wishing I could disappear into the earth. But the matriarch of my family had strict instructions for the kids: when elders visited we were to sit around looking very respectful and keep our mouths shut. 'You better fatten her up a bit or no one will marry her,' another hag told my mother, prodding her in the rib. 'And feed her well. You look like you eat up all the food in the house,' another chortled.

I was in the bathroom shivering in the cold while taking my bath one day, when I had the first proper sighting of my twin assets. There, definitely, were the twin signs that I could still have a life and not be relegated to being a matron. When I wore my tight, bright red T-shirt that evening, I could distinctly see my most prized possessions from under the fabric and it thrilled me to bits. Amma's hawk eyes caught the new addition on my T-shirt front too, thank God, because she looked at me in amusement and said, 'You need to wear a bra now.' Thankfully, she could not see my heart soar and do a celebratory back flip. Unable to contain my excitement about this miracle I did attempt to sidle up to my elder sister, just under two years older, and declared I was going to wear a bra soon but she turned up her nose and swept away in a cloud of her own beauty. Kid sisters are a pain sometimes and I was definitely one to her. I once wore her bra which was drying in the bathroom and was pained that it hung loose because I possessed nothing that could fill up the bra cup.

Amma landed up at school at 5:30 p.m. the next day and took the elder sibling and me to Kalpana Bra Shoppe, situated, unfortunately, right next to the school. I grew up in a small suburban Mumbai town and in those days the place had just this one bra shop. In fact, it was the pride of our town. Amma liked the store because it was also cheap and cheerful, even though its owner, Hasmukhbhai, looked chronically morose. Not many people seemed to be buying bras that evening and Hasmukhbhai was reading a newspaper while his two adolescent shop assistants sat around swatting flies and giggling over some private joke.

'*Kaise ho, behen*?' Hasmukhbhai said upon noticing us three.

'*Theek hain*,' Amma replied, pulling me out from where I was trying to hide, behind her considerable backside. '*Iska size ka bawdy dyo*,' she said loudly, pointing at an unsuspecting me as I cowered in the unexpected spotlight, in my grey school pinafore.

Instantly, three pairs of eyes – Hasmukhbhai's heavy-lidded, barely open eyes and two pairs of very excited and curious adolescent eyes – zoomed in on my chest and stayed there, sizing me up. 'Size twenty-eight,' Hasmukhbhai said with quiet confidence. Having seen any number of teenage girls who were dragged to his store by their mothers, Hasmukhbhai was a veteran at sizing up girls. Literally. One look and he had demolished my thirty-four-sized dreams, cutting it down to a pathetic twenty-eight, and now I had two men, visibly amused at my poor performance on the cup-size front, pulling out bras from glass shelves on which they sat, row upon row of them.

My first bra-buying expedition ended with me triumphantly carrying back two Sonari bras – one black and one white – and spending the better part of an hour trying them on and admiring myself in the mirror until Amma hollered and said it was time for me to do the evening dishes.

What I had not realized was that my bra-buying mission had been witnessed by a couple of boys from my class who happened to pass by Kalpana Bra Shoppe at the seminal moment the shop assistants were waving bras in front of my eyes, and the scene was duly relayed to the rest of the pimple-ridden boys in class. The result was that no sooner had I entered the classroom the next day, following my conical bra which announced my arrival, than thirty-five pairs of eyes swooped down on the sight and sniggered. Not that I did not enjoy the attention, but I was not sure why they were sniggering. Was it my size twenty-eight?

Cut to the modern-day bra-buying expedition and the situation is much different.

'It is all about being beautiful on the inside. If you are beautiful inside, then you look beautiful outside.' I remember a particularly obnoxious eighteen-something, stick-insect in a bikini spouting this rather weighty life lesson while standing with her bony hip thrust out, pouting at the judges at a beauty contest.

But what if your inside is as droopy as your morale at fifty? There is something about that figure (pun intended) that sets off a silent alarm amongst the bravest of women. It is the end of perky and the beginning of a free fall. Literally.

When the aforementioned chill in the bedroom began looking like a permanent affair, I decided to undertake some damage control. Some furtive googling and reading of innumerable glossy magazines while getting my hair coloured at the salon, and I knew why things were so droopy back home. I needed some uplifting action, both on the outside and the inside, a beauteous soul with a Botox-induced grimace, who doubles up as Agony Aunt in a glossy, informed me. 'Men love racy lingerie and women who want to keep their men should do well to remember that,' she added grimly.

And so, I trundled off to the mall a few months ago, keeping the operation a secret so that I could surprise Hassled Harry with my racy new persona. It was sale season, and that being the only time when I could buy anything from a mall without worrying myself into a nervous state, I walked bravely into the fancy showroom of a much-coveted lingerie brand, my insides quaking. It did not help that men in all shapes and sizes hung around the store, following their wives/girlfriends like baa lambs. They all had one thing in common – their eyeballs looked like they would pop out of their peepers any moment.

I cannot understand this sort of community buying of lingerie. I cannot understand how or why men – young, old, ancient, debauched, or decent – walk into lingerie shops and ask for lingerie for their significant other of the moment.

'What would you like to see today, sir?' I once witnessed a brassy, blonde sales assistant in Boston asking a fat slob who was loitering at Victoria's Secret, glassy-eyed.

'Oh, why don't you show me some G-strings? What kind would you recommend?' I fled the scene right after I heard the said blonde tell him, 'Come on over, hon. I will show you G-strings that will have her swooning.'

Right here, in India too, I have seen this intimate domestic scene unfolding many times. You walk into a store to buy your staple nude T-shirt bra and inevitably you will run into couples who are jointly buying her underwear and the air is full of, '*Yeh wala kaisa rahega, jaanu*?' or 'Don't be naughty, sweetie. I can't wear crotchless panties to work!'

Within five minutes of entering the shop and being given pitying once-overs by the lovelies who double up as store assistants ('How can you walk into our store with a thirty-six-plus-plus requirement?'), my spirits and my breasts drooped in disappointment as I realized this was going to be more challenging than I had imagined. Will somebody please tell me why a woman needs to wear a balcony on her bra? I know the bit about the prince using the beauteous Rapunzel's hair to clamber up her balcony, but a balcony bra seems to me a bit weird. Then there were balconette bras (half a balcony is a balconette), and demis, strapless, multi-ways, racerbacks, and underwired bras in orange, yellow, candyfloss pink, midnight blue and black. And there were sheer lacy ones, and satin bras with matching itsy-bitsy undies that had cute little bows in the centre. Then there were the bras that were less bras and more weapons of torture: push-up, extreme push-up, side-push bras, all designed to create the illusion of being a well-stacked woman, if you know what I mean. Herein lie two questions that have always haunted me. One, while I have coveted an underwired bra for the longest time, does the damn thing not poke the Significant Other? Two, if you do land a man, thanks to the size of your twin assets, what happens to the relationship when he eventually sees it was all an illusion and much padding? Will it take the stuffing out of the twosome?

I must confess that at one point during my visit to the lingerie store I did eye a certain racy number in a shade of red that would have driven a bull to desperation, but my assets warned me that wearing a feather on the breast might be good neither for my professional life nor my personal. The Significant Other, I suspect, would spend the night sneezing from feather-induced allergy. And so, with my considerable assets feeling rather deprived and unadorned, I beat it from the store, feeling the sniggers from the bunnies, sorry...the lovelies. My assets were clearly non-performing assets, given that they could not be accommodated in a balcony, pushed up, pushed down, shown off, maximized, or minimized.

My visit to the lingerie shop did not have the desired effect on my marital life. Having declined a salesgirl's saucy suggestion that I set fire to the bedroom with a pair of cute, crotchless panties – I have spent my entire adult life wearing practical, entirely boring nude, white, and black bras and panties – I was out of the door as if my tail was on fire. I have since taken to buying my bras online and am glad Hassled Harry can't see very much in the dark.

THE D WORD

I DON'T KNOW WHAT it is about entering my fifties, but I am now, finally, in a place where I am happy to own up to almost all the things that I hated to admit before. Including the dreaded D word. D for divorced and damned. When my first marriage to my college sweetheart ended up at the divorce court I was devastated, guilt-stricken and embarrassed, and spent over a decade avoiding the people I love, simply because I did not want to discuss my divorce. Or even admit to it. The D word had me skulking around and avoiding social contact for almost fifteen years of my life.

Here is how a typical social interaction in those days went:

'Hello, Sudha, wonderful to see you at this wedding. Been a long time. And where is XYZ [Spouse No. 1]? You both should visit us one of these days!'

Me (stuttering and stammering a bit): 'Yes, been a long time. I have been caught up with a lot of work. You know how it is.' Scoots the scene immediately.

Or, long-time acquaintance at a neighbourhood mall or bookstore:

'Hello, Sudha. Good to run into you. Look at your daughter, how tall she has become. Where is your husband? Left him alone at home to do the dishes, *haan*?'

Me: 'Lovely to see you. Yes, children grow up so fast, isn't it? All well, I hope. See you around. Bye!' Scoots, leaving perplexed acquaintance behind.

I'm not sure if this happens to the male species but a woman faces this all the time! In the years that I was trying to raise my daughter, keep a job and keep my head above water with all the things going on in my life, the thing that bothered me the most was the constant ducking behind pillars or disappearing from the scene because I did not want to answer one more husband question.

The shadow of my 'husband' followed me wherever I went, and I was too much of a coward to stand up straight and say that there was, in fact, no husband. We were divorced and happy with our single status.

I'm sure there are divorced women who, like me, have gone through the trauma of socializing without being accompanied by the spouse. I have walked into a roomful of married men and women and seen the womenfolk, till then busy gossiping amongst themselves, perk up and make a beeline for their husbands. Can't trust a single woman with the husband, can we? She might be on the prowl.

And I have seen the men suck up their bellies and broaden their chests before moving in for the kill: 'Hi Sudha, long time no see. You are looking better than ever. Getting younger by the day! What's the secret? We must catch up. Why don't you drop by at the office one of these days? Or, better still, why don't we grab coffee post work?' And they think this is subtle. My years in journalism following my divorce was a study in avoiding all kinds of important male executives and business leaders who think women – single, married, or divorced – are easy meat. The number of 'special stories' I passed up in those years are many because they came along with invitations for coffee and conversation from sundry men in the corporate sector! When a woman gets divorced, no matter what her age, shape, size, or inclination, word gets around super fast. And sundry members of the male species, no matter what their age, shape, or size, move in to try their luck.

The D word is the worst when it comes to the family and during our endless festivals, weddings, and the like. For long, lonely years following my divorce and my remarriage, I was almost a ghost – present on everyone's mind but never in person – because I did not have the courage to face the judgement in the eyes of all and sundry. And I did not want to embarrass my parents who were devastated by my divorce from a man they had grown to love like one of their own.

Then, two years ago, finally, at the ripe age of fifty, things changed miraculously. I woke up one day and decided that I have just this one life to live and I was done with spending it in the shadows. Suddenly, I was able to make eye contact with my broken marriage and make peace with myself for God-alone-knows-what crimes I imagined I had committed. I am finally comfortable acknowledging that I was married before and that I have found love all over again in a wonderful man who cherishes me.

Now, when the inevitable questions about the former spouse come up when I run into common friends, I have this to say: 'Oh, I thought you already knew. XYZ and I have been divorced for ages. We have both remarried since. Why don't you drop in one of these days? You must come over and say hi to Hassled Harry.' I hate to see the discomfiture of the poor folk who are at the receiving end of this information. *But better them than me*, I think to myself.

Over the years I have realized one thing: there is no such thing as a perfect life, a perfect family, or a perfect anything. We all come into this world flawed and full of imperfections and the sooner we embrace them, the better.

Looking back, I don't know why I went through the agonizing few years of self-blame and suffered the endless guilt that eventually affected my well-being.

Divorces are not easy on anyone. Not on the couple who promised to stay together till their last breath and not on the children they brought into the world. When we decided to go our separate ways – not because we did not love each other but because we had grown up into different people – our biggest worry was our daughter. There were enough people who blamed and warned us that we had caused our daughter immeasurable harm with our selfish decision, and for the longest time I stewed in guilt over that.

When we decided to part ways and remain friends, we made a pact that no matter what happened in our future lives and no matter whoever else became part of our lives, our daughter would remain at the centre of our universe. We have kept that promise. And our daughter now has two sets of doting parents, instead of one.

I wish I had had the awareness all those years ago when Amma raged, raved and ranted about my decision to marry my college sweetheart and eventually took to her bed in grief when I refused to relent on my decision. I was in love and the hormones were raging, and he made me feel special like nothing and nobody ever had before, and I wanted to revel in that feeling: love and be loved. Amma would have none of it because she feared what society would have to say about my inter-religious marriage. I appealed to my beloved Achan, the one who always stood up for me, but he chose to stay neutral this time, maintaining he was OK with whatever Amma decided, and, eventually, in the face of their refusal to see the situation from my perspective, I simply went against their wishes and got married to the boy I loved.

When that marriage came undone and we decided to go our separate ways, Amma grieved again, this time for the man I was walking away from. He was a kind human being and a loving husband, she said, forgetting that she had objected to our union in the first place, pointing out that I would never find anyone else who would care for me that much. She took to her bed again and, this time, it was she who appealed to my father to intervene. I still remember the summer afternoon in their bedroom, the late afternoon sun streaming in from their garden, and Achan looking at me with just a hint of sorrow in his eyes, saying, 'Every marriage has its ups and downs. The answer is not to flee but stay and resolve the problems.' I never listened to them.

It has been decades since then and both of us have moved on, finding loving partners who have helped us grow and flourish, and our daughter has grown up to be a kind young woman who has embarked on her own journey of discovery.

It is only now that I can claim to understand just a little bit of what my parents went through when I announced my undying love for a boy I had known for just under a year. I was barely twenty-one and had lived a sheltered existence in our tight-knit family where every activity – picnics, movies, or that rare meal out – was with the family. Growing up in a small town in suburban Mumbai, with its suffocating social mores, meant I had had little or nothing to do with boys and was clueless about their world. To be told that I would go off with a person they did not even know must have been the most frightening prospect for my parents. And even if I still feel sometimes that their acceptance could have made the initial years of my marriage much happier, I understand today that they were simply trying to protect their child and save her from potential hurt.

When I hang out with my fledgling now and have one of our rare chats about life, love, and everything in between, I sometimes feel a pain in my heart that I suspect only mothers can understand. Sometimes I am terrified of what the future holds for us. Someday, soon, she will meet a boy she will fall in love with and marry. And while that thought fills me with joy, it is also pure terror in the darkness of the night when I worry about things that can go wrong. What if the boy she marries turns out to be a wife-beater or an alcoholic? What if he emotionally abuses her? What if he is unkind and thoughtless? What if he demeans her, puts her down, and kills her spirit? God, have I brought her up with enough confidence to share her predicament with her parents? Have I told her enough that no matter how painful or embarrassing a situation, she can come to me to unburden and seek help? When I see her today, happily going about her life with a bounce in her step, I send up a silent prayer and hope desperately that Amma's God, the one who, she says, looks after all of us, will watch over my girl, too.

Touch wood!

NEW KIDS ON THE BLOCK

PARDON ME FOR SAYING this but the world is going to the dogs. And cats. And to guinea pigs and rabbits too. Animals are taking over the world and they want all of it, including the very chairs on which we sit. Literally.

The other day I was visiting a close friend and just as I rested my posterior on a rather jaded chair, a fat cat waddled across the room and plonked itself on my feet. I cringed and sent up a silent scream since I was aware this was a family of cat lovers and I did not want to upset them by creating a racket or kicking the cat on the rump.

I fidgeted this way and that, trying to dislodge said cat from my freshly pedicured feet, but this was a cat with a mind of its own; the more I tried to dislodge it, the firmer it seemed to become in its resolve to stay put. Eventually, when the imaginary (hopefully) ticks from its body started crawling up my leg, I weakly asked the family members, sitting with somewhat strained expressions on their faces, if there was a reason the cat would not get off my feet.

'Actually, you are sitting on Queen's favourite chair. She is very possessive about her chair,' the daughter of the house said, indulgently.

'Oh. I had no idea. Do you want me to vacate the seat for her?'

'That would be lovely!' the lady of the house chimed in. 'Queenie, say thank you to Auntie Sudha. Naughty girl, I did not see you say hello to her.'

Barely had I gotten up from the chair when the fat cat stretched in a leisurely manner, gave itself a good shake and jumped onto the chair, from where she gave me a glare much like my headmistress did when she caught me clambering over the school compound to get myself a forbidden treat of cream-filled buns from the bakery outside the gate.

I am not sure what I had done to earn her ire but the 'catmistress' kept a stern eye on me for most part of the rather strained visit. I have a confession to make. I am the queen of paranoia and, like my mother, health magazines are my favourite lunchtime reads. I am a walking-talking encyclopaedia of illnesses and I know the symptoms and home remedies for a hundred ailments and, so, I firmly believe that cat hair, like horse hair, causes all sorts of dangerous illnesses.

My allergy to cats also comes from the many cat stories my grandma and grand-aunts would narrate during our annual visits to Kerala. The cats in these stories were greedy and shrewd like foxes, and they were always scheming. One of my grand-aunts had this hilarious story about a cat which had somehow wormed its way into our home and every afternoon as the family snoozed after lunch, it would jump down the chimney and eat up all the fish curry that she had kept aside for dinner. The grandpa loved his fish curry and rice and did not take kindly to being denied his favourite dinner.

One day, in a fit of anger, he picked up the cat, tied it up in a gunny bag, and travelled some twenty kilometres, crossing over to the other side of the Lord Canolly Canal, where he set it free and headed home for lunch. Imagine his surprise when the first thing he set eyes on, upon entering the house, was the very same exiled cat hanging outside the kitchen from where emanated the glorious smell of fried fish. The family lore goes that the stand-off between the old man and the cat went on till the very end. It is not clear who kicked the bucket first: man or cat. The legacy they left, of course, is a family with a lifelong allergy to cats.

Meanwhile, back to the visit to my friend. Lunch was excruciatingly traumatic because that was also when eight other cats came visiting – let me correct myself ... I was visiting, they lived there. Apparently, the cat family converges at the dining table daily to exchange notes about their various pre-lunch activities. It was bizarre to say the least, but I had lunch with nine cats and two adoring mistresses who plied them with the choicest pieces of fried fish while I sulked like a neglected baby. What I especially took umbrage to were the constant references to 'Auntie Sudha' who, they insisted, had got them the most delicious chocolate cake ever. I like chocolate cake. I really do. And I was looking forward to a slice of that cake, especially after the ordeal with crafty cats. To cut a long story short, I cut short my visit, miffed at being gypped out of my share of cake. I still remember the nine gloating cat faces that lined up at the balcony, waving goodbye to me. 'Ask Auntie Sudha to get you pineapple cake next time,' the mistress of the house said to the cat family as I fled the scene.

Don't get me wrong. It is not that I don't like cats or dogs. Growing up, I have had my own share of pets. At the age of eight someone gifted me the cutest puppy in the world and I can safely tell you that I was in love with the little one who was darker than the devil and just a bit bigger than our soap case. He was so tiny that he looked more like a fat rat than a puppy and he could barely walk without tumbling over. I rather creatively named him Kaalu and he became the reason I stopped roaming around like a ragamuffin after school; I came rushing back like a homing pigeon. I fed him all sorts of delicious morsels, gave him my share of Horlicks when Amma was not looking, and I put pink ribbons on his floppy ears. And then my kindness took over and took his poor life.

For as long as I can remember, my mind has been a boiling cauldron of concerns for all things living. I remember chasing away crows that I saw sitting on the back of my grandma's cows, pecking away at them. I once bunged a badminton racket at a lizard when it was about to pounce on an insect on our bedroom wall and I got whacked by Amma because the racket broke the light bulb and we had to spend the night in darkness.

Coming back to my Kaalu story: one day I came home and saw him going around in crazy circles chasing his own tail, trying to scratch it. *Maybe he is itchy because I have not given him a bath*, I thought to myself, and, overcome with guilt, I picked up the li'l baby, marched him to the bathroom and proceeded to give him a good few dunks in a bucket of water, after which I scrubbed him with soap and dunked him again. Happy at a good job done, I let him scurry off to his favourite spot under the sofa. When we woke up the next morning Kaalu had a fever, and by evening he was dead. Saying goodbye to that bundle of joy broke my heart and I put him to rest in our garden. Achan allowed me to plant a rose bush over his grave. I wonder sometimes if it was the bath that took his life.

I have had other pets, too, including a tortoise that lived in the water tank in our garden. He was much like me, silent and shy, and when I returned from school I would take him out and let him hang around with us in the garden. Soon I felt I had forged a bond with him because he would occasionally look up at me with wide open eyes, as if he wanted to say something to me. Panic-stricken, I would imagine he was hungry and throw him pieces of bread or crumbs of roti. I imagined he was in pain and would try to pat him and he would promptly retreat into his shell and remain like that till we kids left him alone. When we returned home from school one day, the tortoise was gone. We searched for him high and low in our tiny walled cottage. Eventually, we found the tunnel he had dug in Achhan's rose garden, which opened on the other side of the compound. He had escaped. I still wonder what may have happened to him. Did he get eaten by a nasty dog? Did someone have roast tortoise for dinner? Did the circling hawks swoop down and have him for a good meal?

Did I tell you about the time the kids in our railway colony had a tiger cub (Or maybe it was a leopard? I'm not sure anymore.) for a pet? God's truth. This is the whole truth and nothing but the truth. In the early 1970s, a friend's father – a motorman – was plying a goods train on the Ghats section (I don't remember where exactly, though) when the train's headlights detected some movement on the railway tracks that lay ahead. He braked in time and went over to investigate. To his surprise it turned out to be a cub the size of a cat. He could not bring himself to leave it on the tracks to either be mowed down by a train or be eaten by another animal, and so the kindly man got it home.

I can safely say that not one kid in the railway colony needed to go out to play in the maidan outside for weeks after Shera's arrival because we simply could not have enough of him. He was the cutest thing and would jump from lap to lap, licking our faces and hands as we fed him milk in a saucer, and allowed him to chase us in the compound of our friend's home. He was our joint property and we apportioned time so that each of us got to cuddle him and lap up all his love.

I am not sure how long after his arrival our tiny pal started outgrowing our laps and feeling too heavy in our arms. The little guy was growing up fast and was almost as big as a dog before we knew it. I remember his claws felt sharp when he chased us playfully and swiped at us with his paws. And then, one day, disaster struck. Dusk had fallen, and we were saying goodbyes to Shera when there was a knock on the door. A group of policemen from the police station right across our house stood at the door.

'Is there a tiger in the house?' one of them rasped.

'It is our pet and it is a small cub,' we chorused, fearful suddenly for our not-so-tiny friend who came bounding out from his makeshift cage, peering curiously at the visitors. The cops then huddled and ordered that the owner of the house must report to the police station when he returned from work.

We got home from school the next evening and having tossed our school bags inside, rushed off as usual for our tryst with Shera. He was not there, nor was his cage. Our friend's mom sat in the garden, looking forlorn. When she saw us she burst out sobbing, saying the police had come that afternoon and taken him away. We ran across to the police station when we heard this and cried, implored, shouted at the policemen but they were unmoved.

According to the rules nobody could keep wildlife in their homes, they said. Our little friend had been sent away to a zoo and they refused to say anything more. In many ways that day was the end of our innocence because we realized that we humans can put a tag on any being and treat them according to our perception. Our cub was the gentlest baby that we knew but they chose to call him a wild animal and put him away where he could not harm anyone.

Coming back to the topic of pets, I have an urgent query: are dogs our new kids? I have a lot of friends who used to have kids but when their progeny grew up and flew the nest, they decided to fill up their empty nest with dogs. They became dog parents.

Here is my theory about why dogs are our new kids. When the kids are growing up they get expensive Adidas sneakers, hideous below-the-knee branded cargoes, and even more hideous superman tees, hot pants, wedges, and so on. When they leave to build their own nests, the only way bereft parents can get over their weaning woes is to attach themselves to other beings: dogs. It helps that dogs are way more loyal and won't ask to use your credit card to buy the latest gizmo.

Next, these newbie dog parents spend their days being dragged along by their dog children on their morning walks. The other part of the day, of course, is spent cooking for them, taking them out for spa treats, shopping for cute booties, and boring unsuspecting friends with stories of their dog's brilliance. Same as we used to do with kids, in the good old days.

Why, there is this friend of mine who insists that his dog, Buster, is as intelligent as the couple's kids who studied at Harvard. 'He follows world news as intently as we do. In fact, he gets a part of the newspaper when we are reading the newspaper in the morning,' he said to me recently.

'How clever,' I said weakly, hoping that Buster, who sat on the sofa across from me, never came visiting. I have nothing against dogs, but I draw the line at sharing my newspaper with them. Why, I never even share my newspaper with my spouse. I am possessive of my newspaper and refuse to let man or dog take it away from me.

My dog-parent friends also have dog kids with attitude. I have this smart friend who is in the food business and brings home the finest cheeses and other gourmet stuff from around the world for her family. Turns out her pet dog has fine taste too: my friend swears that the dog practically sneers if offered a piece of Indian cheese while the family is nibbling on artisanal Italian or French cheese and sipping wine. Give her a bit of blue cheese, however, and she is more than happy to polish it off in the blink of an eye, my friend says, her eyes twinkling with pride.

Maybe it is just me, but I can't get over the fact that half my friends these days roam around zombie-like;

they are sleep deprived because of the dog's snores. One of my friends recently fell out of her own bed thanks to the Labrador who sleeps between the couple and has Restless Leg Syndrome!

I am all for sharing the planet, but Hassled Harry's snores keep me awake half the night. I don't need myself no dogs to hog the quilt, claim my side of the bed, or snore in my face. When I say I need more action in bed, I definitely don't mean this.

Dogs may be man's best friends, but I take exception when they come and sniff at my nether regions. I have lost count of the number of times I have gone into rigor mortis when this has happened to me at sundry dog homes. Picture this: there you are, in your stylish new threads, standing tall in your insanely glamorous red stilettos and suddenly you feel some movement in your nethers. You look down and screech in terror. There is a dog in your crotch. Literally. The owner's dog has somehow managed to stand up on its hind legs and is attempting to nuzzle your unmentionables and the whole world is watching.

'Don't worry about Sheba. She is just smelling your crotch to make friends with you,' the mistress of the house purrs, passing around plates of hors d'oeuvres, blissfully unaware that half a dozen eyes are now trained on the above-mentioned part of my anatomy. In a saner world I used to know other ways of striking friendships. I can safely say this experience is way more embarrassing than another friend's dog that spends his time trying to mate with the sofa leg!

As for me, I am through with holding my breath and keeping my mouth shut at the homes of my dog-parent friends so that I don't accidentally swallow the clouds of dog hair that languorously float past my face. I have fewer friends now and every day I send up a silent prayer, fervently hoping that the remaining few of my friends don't get it into their heads to acquire dogs. There used to be a time when childless couples were harassed beyond measure with tips on begetting children and even shamed for opting out of parenthood. Dog-shaming has replaced this phenomenon now and I am frequently advised to get myself a dog so I am not as boring. Besides, I am told I can join the fun dog vacations that these folks push off to.

If company is what I miss, I would rather check myself into the loony bin. Just saying.

MULTITASKING MAVEN

LOLLING ON THE SOFA the other evening, eating a slice of papaya and reading the newspaper, I feel that familiar restlessness taking charge. I turn a page and try to focus on the news item but the image of the cheesecake sitting in the fridge floats in out of nowhere and, no matter how much I try to focus, it refuses to go away. The headlines and text in the news item pale into insignificance compared to the temptation of the strawberry cheesecake that beckons me like a secret lover who won't take no for an answer.

I surrender to temptation after ten minutes of demurring; soon, I am at the fridge door, digging into the cheesecake as if my life depends on it. Barely have I downed about eight sizeable bites of the cake when my eyes land on the far corner of the fridge. I spot alien life. It's grey in colour and resembles one of those molecular gastronomy ice creams or sorbets – dark, mysterious, and hanging over the container like a cloud. Cheesecake forgotten, I zero in on the mysterious something to find out if indeed my cook (who can't cook to save her life) has taken to either molecular gastronomy or exorcism (I would think her more capable of the latter).

I peer into the swirling darkness of the cloud, but that gives me no clue about the identity of the dish. I bring it close to my nose – the unidentifiable mass smells like my idea of hell but still no clue about what it is. I pick up a spoon and, with a silent prayer, poke into it. The spoon sinks into its gooey surface which I scoop out and, upon closer examination, it turns out to be the remnants of last month's tomato salsa, the one I had instructed my cook to store in my sea-green ceramic salsa container.

Why is the salsa in a steel bowl when there was a designated container for it? And, more importantly, where is my sea-green ceramic container? I smell a rat; the container is probably in the garbage bin in a million pieces and the cook has conveniently forgotten to tell me. I need solid evidence before I can confront the cat. Hot on her trail, I rush to check the bin under the kitchen sink and make eye contact with the following: three dish rags that require washing; two of my dessert platters from last week's dinner, chipped and hidden away from my eyes; one broom that has long seen its expiry date but has still not been discarded. 'No wonder the house looks poorly swept most days,' I mutter, sniffing in disgust and possibly because of the fumes of the fossilized salsa in the fridge.

'If this is the state of affairs under the kitchen sink, I must find out what is in the waste bins in the other rooms and corners of the house,' I tell myself, and rush to have a look. Under the sofa I find the length of red silk fabric that I had bought to make a blouse for my new saree; it had since disappeared mysteriously and, after searching high and low, I had resigned myself to never finding it, telling myself I had probably left it behind at the store.

Wait a minute, what happened to the saree that goes with the blouse? Thirty minutes of frantic searching and piling up the innards of my wardrobe on my bed later, I realize the saree is at the laundry shop for ironing. Quick bath and out the door with the cooker lid and mixer, both of which need fixing.

Now that I am out, I might as well buy some veggies and, oh, those fabulous mushrooms would be perfect for some mushroom cappuccino for dinner. Which means driving four kilometres to the bakery that makes the perfect multigrain bread to go with it. And, if I am eating healthy, might as well make a salad to go with the soup and toast. Quick stopover at the superstore to pick up salad greens, goat cheese and pine nuts.

I have a love-hate relationship with supermarkets and grocery stores. The food aisles, with their abundance of food items from different corners of the world, guilt-trip me about the boring roti-sabzi routine we have at home most days, because I simply cannot be bothered to cook, and, Sarla, the cook, is even more uninspired than I, if that is even possible. The only interesting meals we have are in other people's home or in restaurants, or when Amma comes calling and spoils us rotten.

Grocery shopping is good for my soul, though. They open my eyes to the endless ways I can save my time by not cooking exotic meals with exotic ingredients I can purchase there. I completely lose myself in reading the instructions on the meal-in-five-minutes bottles and jars, and I am amazed at the smart men and women who write the boring instructions in a manner that is so interesting that hundreds and thousands of consumers take the packets home to feed their families. I would rather spend money on buying a good book, I tell myself, and instantly feel happy about my money-saving self. And about my book-loving self. Besides, by not buying those things packed in paper or, worse, plastic, I am also saving the environment, and so I also admire my conscious-citizen self.

On the way out of the mall I pass by the salon and remember that I need to get my roots touched up and the chin waxed because I suspect the spouse is beginning to look rather pained that instead of his super sexy wife, here's a witch in residence. OK, not really. I don't think there exists a man these days who notices how the wife looks. They are all either too busy admiring their own biceps or busy watching cricket on the phone. Or, going by the number of American marriages that break up owing to social media faux pas, the men are too busy sexting to notice the bitter half's chin hair, even if it is glinting nastily in the evening light.

Salons are strange places these days. I go in and ask for a wax and am met with the following question: 'Ma'am, chocolate?'

'Err, no. I don't want chocolate. I'm dieting. I want a wax.'

'Ma'am, do you want a chocolate wax or an ordinary wax?'

And I thought chocolates were for eating!

The barely-eighteen therapist, however, patiently explains with a barely concealed sneer that nobody really uses ordinary wax anymore. Chocolate wax moisturizes and pampers the skin (also socks you for your last rupee, as I find out) and is a mild bleach as well.

Can I also lick it off, I want to ask her, but good sense prevails and I surrender myself to a chocolate wax. Come to think of it, it is a good experience because the aroma of warm chocolate takes away the pain of waxing, which, incidentally, is almost as bad, possibly, as being sawed slowly into two pieces. Not that it has ever kept me away from being waxed, though. The chocolate wax made me ponder about other potential uses of chocolate. Can we, for instance, have a chocolate swimming pool? Will that make it irresistible for me to go for a swim? Or, can we have a chocolate treadmill? Or a made-of-chocolate personal trainer? The mind boggles at the possibilities.

An hour in the salon later, with newly acquired dark brown tresses bouncing gaily in the air, the thought strikes me that, since I am looking gorgeous this might be the time to meet up with the girls who are always ready to mingle. And also finish a quick business meeting that I have been putting off because I was between root touch-ups. It is half-past six when the realization dawns that the spouse is due to get home in an hour and there is no dinner in sight. But hey, this is fabulous hair day and never mind slogging in the kitchen for mushroom cappuccino, salad and garlic bread. Why reinvent the wheel, or, in this case, the mushroom cappuccino, when it can be found in an elegant restaurant? Spouse, forever martyred from eating the endless unimaginative meals conjured up by Sarla, is more than happy to dine out.

Fabulous hair day makes for a happy meal, especially if it involves decadent dessert and a movie at the end of it that features King Khan. It is well past midnight when we totter home, tired and happy. I still have to figure out where my sea-green salsa container went, but that can wait until tomorrow.

MY BIG FAT FOMO

WILL SOMEONE PLEASE TELL me I am not the only fifty-year-old suffering from FOMO? At the crack of dawn every morning, even before I have relieved my overfull bladder, I reach blindly for my smartphone to check what is happening on FB. And, man, there is always a whole lot going on there. Enough to keep me from going back for a quick cuddle with the Significant Other who is snoring away. Instead, I sneak out of the room with my phone and sit on the sofa, hungrily lapping up what the world did while I was asleep.

And before I know it, the clock strikes six and I scramble to brush and don my walking gear to head out the door for an hour's walk. I take my phone along in a sling bag across my shoulder because the smart app on it tells me how many steps I have clocked. The real reason I sneak the phone along, however, is so that I can check Instagram and Twitter and take pictures of random birds, bees, flowers, and such others that I can load on my social media handles during the day, so that the equally random people who check out my posts can eat their heart out over my enviable life.

Oh, she lives in a gated society with lush greenery around her, they probably think to themselves, admiring the video of the peacock that comes calling in my backyard every morning, pecking away at God-alone-knows-what it is that showers down from the badam trees in my backyard. They have no idea that the hysterical calls of the peacocks – I would sound like that if somebody came after me with a butcher's knife – keep me awake half the night. Some days I am most tempted to open the window and bung a stone at whichever gang of stray dogs is holding their private orchestra under my bedroom window. Only, I would rather suffer the racket caused by them than face the music from the clutch of rabid animal lovers in the neighbourhood who go around preaching love for animals and treat human beings like inanimate objects to be trampled on. Oh well, it takes all kinds to make this wonderful world of ours and I am all for coexistence. I can live and share the planet with as many dogs as it can bring on, so long as they don't bite my backside. Very painful, I can tell you, from having been bitten thrice on the aforementioned part of the anatomy.

Coming back to social media, though, I wonder if I have enough meat to sue the smart fellas who invented Facebook, Instagram and Twitter, for my acute case of

Fear Of Missing Out. Tell me if I'm overreacting but after an hour of looking at the happening lives of various people that I know on Facebook in various parts of the world, I end up feeling like the worst loser to have walked this earth. I am done with social media images of loved-up couples sitting by the sea watching glorious sunsets, glamorous women in designer teeny-weeny things flaunting mojitos and pouting into the cameras over lunch at restaurants where celebrity chefs sit down to chat with them.

Then, there are videos of young mothers cuddling their babies in bed and talking about the pure joy of raising their chubby cherubs. Heck, when I was twenty-four I was so hassled trying to give the baby her bath, rustling up lunch for the family, and catching the 9:45 a.m. train to work that I certainly had no time to roll around in bed in pink-and-white coordinated mom-and-baby pyjamas, posing for the phone camera to record the bonding session. Come to think of it, there were no mobile phones back then. In fact, if I were to search, I would find very few pictures of mine from my child-rearing days when my hair permanently stood on end like a frightened porcupine, because of the mountain of chores I had to wade through every day. I had no wish to capture that look to scare away future generations. Thank God, Mark Zuckerberg was not born back then, or I would have the additional pressure of posting on FB among the hundred other things I had to accomplish in twenty-four hours.

Every morning, as I struggle to stay put on my chair and get started with my writing, I am tempted to check my FB account. I resist initially but not being as determined as the successful women that I write about in my books, I find myself on FB in about twenty minutes. And there they are, pictures of girls who go on vacations together to lie on the beach in Bali, cavort in Capri, watch films and beautiful people in Cannes, and do the salsa with handsome hunks in Spain. Ever noticed how perfect they look, those nymph-like creatures, some of them friends of mine who don't mind blowing a few lakhs for a week's holiday? Their hair is impeccable even on the beach, their arms toned, their abs will put Salman Khan to shame, and, as they gaze out at the world from behind the trendiest pairs of aviators ever made, they have little idea they have ruined my morning cuppa.

Worse still are the show-offs in their workout gear, who run, kickbox, or practice martial arts and such other mind- and body-bending stuff; this breed seems to have taken on the responsibility of single-mindedly making the rest of humanity feel slovenly and lazy for not hitting the ground running and notching up miles on the treadmill or bicycle. Some of them put up statistics of their milestones, their future goals, and the number of calories they burnt or saved on a particular day by sheer dint of their discipline; I usually happen to read this at the very moment I am popping my seventh Parle-G biscuit into my mouth, along with sugary tea, or demolishing the last bit of the ten-inch, pan-crust, cheese-stuffed pizza from the previous night.

Occasionally, my heart yearns for the stuff I see on FB. *I want a gang of gal pals to travel the world with, I want a man to woo me with chocolate, cake, and flowers, and I want to post it all on FB*, I tell myself, sighing loudly so the Old Man sitting with his head immersed in the newspaper knows how miffed I am with his unromantic ways. A woman needs the occasional PDA, even if it is just for an envy-inducing selfie. And then I quickly tell myself that it's better to be updated on what is happening in the real world than eat my heart out over things I can't help.

Only, the real world too seems to be full of things that I missed. Tried reading the newspapers recently? I am beginning to think there are no ordinary mortals doing ordinary things for their living and looking like ordinary mortals, with moles and warts, big noses, and hair on their chin. Instead, the newspapers that I read are full of perfect-looking people in designer clothes, sipping wine, and nibbling at gourmet morsels at soirees to raise funds for the underprivileged.

In addition to stalking minor and major celebs outside their homes, salons, and at airports, the media has now decided the world needs to see filmstars preening in their workout gear. Open the newspaper on any day and you are likely to be treated to the sight of Kylie Jenner and others of her ilk in body-con outfits that show off every bone in their bodies.

My FOMO seems to be getting worse by the day. In the last few months the list of things I want to do has grown really long. To begin with I want to be a radio jockey. I know a couple of them personally and they have the best lives, meeting with all sorts of interesting folks and having half of the city clamouring to be invited on their talk shows. I also want to become an actor. For as far long as I can remember I have dreamt of being on the silver screen, singing soulful songs with Manoj Kumar, Rajendra Kumar, Dharmendra for some time, then Kumar Gaurav, followed by the love of my life, Shah Rukh Khan. It is altogether another matter that these days that dream has been considerably downgraded. I am now willing to even play SRK's sister. But, no, I will not play his mother. Even fifty-year-olds have their dignity. And while we are on the topic I would like to be Kangana Ranaut too. I like how sassy she is and how her newsworthiness goes up exponentially with every outrageous new disclosure she makes. When I say outrageous things, even if they be God's truth, I only get shushed by the daughter and the spouse. 'You don't have to verbalize everything that comes to your mind, Mom,' the daughter says and Hassled Harry nods in complete agreement.

When I get time off from being actor and RJ, I want to try my hand at pottery. And I think I can be the best Latin American dancer on the subcontinent (when I am home alone and bored to death, I stand in front of the mirror and pretend I am one). I want to be a singer too, and when I see pictures of women who abandon the chaos of city life to live in splendid isolation in the hills, where they hold the most exciting literary salons, I want to do that too. The other day I read about a woman who wore her great-grandmother's wedding saree for her own nuptials and I roundly cursed my mother who, in a fit of mad decluttering of our home, sold her wedding saree to the kabadiwallah for five hundred rupees. Since I have taken the marriage vows twice in the last thirty years, I felt doubly cheated out of the opportunity to be known as the diva who is a restorer of antique sarees.

Then there are full-length articles about India's most-followed celebrity writers who move about in charmed circles with similarly privileged writers and publishers, live in picture-perfect homes where they host their ilk with wine and cheese, and discuss the state of publishing, the next big author they discovered, or the rare talent of one of their sons or daughters, a literary protégé in the making. Or, there are write-ups about high-profile authors who got together to bring out anthologies that they talk about in a tone that clearly implies that if you are one of the miserable ones who did not get invited to contribute to it, you have no business being in the business. Go disappear into your hole is what they want to say.

Newspapers and the media have a social responsibility. If the first thing their product does to unsuspecting readers in the morning is to pull down their spirit and make them feel persecuted and unworthy, they should do well to change what they put in their publications. I begin most of my mornings eating humble pie because I fall into none of the above categories. I am not rich and while I am mildly famous in my own city, I am nowhere near as famous as the folks who flock together for cheese and wine soirees. I am in no anthology or at the cocktail dinners of powerful publishers and authors, even though I have written a clutch of popular books that resonate with readers. I am tired of being the author with no connections with the big bosses of big-ticket lit fests who will not give me the time of the day, leave alone a chance to speak on one of their panels because I am simply too small-town for them.

But heck, I am also the one who gets emails and letters from readers who write to tell me that my books have magically transformed their lives, given them the motivation to carry on despite the hurdles, and taught them to be more compassionate, loving, and positive. I feel grateful to be in their good books, even though I am not in the pages of the newspapers, trying to shoulder my way into a P3 picture. I might not be able to post Insta or FB images of receiving awards, sounding off on the telly, or breaking bread with the bold and the beautiful but I have the pure joy of women approaching me at bookstores, airports, or the neighbourhood mall and telling me they are awaiting my next book so that they can gift it to a beloved daughter, sister, or wife. 'Ma'am, when I read your books I feel you have written it just for me. Your books gave me hope at a time I was really struggling with self-doubt,' one young techie told me some time ago after reading one of my books.

Meanwhile, since I am not busy doing one important thing after the other, I can hang around and enjoy my time, and occasionally watch my pastry-chef daughter bake the most gorgeous cakes and pastries.

Speaking of which, where the hell is my phone? I have to post an image of that cake on Insta. Right now! Mothers get bragging rights, don't they?

1

HAIR ON THE CHIN

IF FIFTY IS THE new forty, then can I please fast forward to seventy? Really fast? Please? Hopefully I will either have ceased by then or have ceased to care about all the stuff that seems to suddenly consume my every waking moment. And believe me, my waking moments are very, very long these days, between the snoring spouse and menopausal hot flashes.

The other day I was raring to go out for a girls' lunch that was finally happening after half a dozen of us women in our fifties were finally done changing plans multiple times. I was beginning to think that we would all be in our graves by the time this lunch happened, when one of them called, screeching into the phone, 'It is all sorted; Amy has found someone to babysit her granddaughter while she has lunch with us on Thursday. Deeps has gone and broken her leg but is coming over with the leg in a cast, and, oh, Sunaina is wondering what to do with her newly retired husband and hinted that she would bring him along. He is a terrible bore and why should we deal with this…' You get the drift.

'OK, OK. I will see you at 1 p.m. sharp, at Diva,' I said hastily. 'And no, I can't pick you up because I don't have a driver and I'll be cabbing it.' Latika is slowly becoming hard of hearing but remains blissfully unaware that she has taken to talking so loudly that the rest of us fear we will soon be deaf as well. Plus, I also got off the phone real quick because I was not about to tell her I had to make a last-minute sprint to my salon to get the hair fixed and my nails polished.

Realization strikes the moment I get off the phone. $#$@S#$%$E! Tomorrow is Thursday and the salon will be closed. There is no way I am going out looking like a witch about to board a broom. I've been putting off going to the salon to get my roots touched up and the crowning glory is now three different shades: white, grey and the colour of straw. I have no clue how the last colour crept into my once-raven locks. Already past four; can I make a quick dash for the salon before it shuts at six?

Grab car key and mad-dash out of the door, driving like the devil is chasing me, to reach at 4:25 p.m. and slump on the salon chair; my regular beauty therapist clucks sympathetically and brings me a cup of tea before proceeding to transform me into the beautiful creature I like to see in the mirror. Yes, yes, I know we have to embrace ourselves and love who we are and the body we have. I could not agree more. But I love my hair dark brown and my nails red, and it is about choice, isn't it? I choose to embrace the dark-haired, nail-polished me. The old man back home often tells me that he loves me as I am and that white hair is graceful on women, but sputters into pained silence when I give him *the* look. If ever I had a last wish it is that I go to my grave with gorgeously blow-dried dark-brown hair. And red nails, if that is not too much to ask. Red lipstick would be the cherry on the cake.

Hair done, I get home and that is when the next struggle begins. Hitting the Big F has, somehow, brought with it this pressing need to go all mod. Out with the 5.5 metre saree and the dupattas that now seem to weigh me down and suck out my oxygen. I want to walk light on this earth and breathe free. A few months ago, I went to Westside during their annual sale (that is the only season I shop considering how expensive things are for a broke author) and the first thing that I set eyes on was this sleeveless blue linen dress with pockets – and I knew it was meant for me. It was almost like how I met the two men in my life. One ex and one current. The moment the eyes met I knew this was the one for me. I never regretted those emotional investment decisions and neither do I regret the little blue dress that I invested in.

I took it to the trial room and got out of the salwar kameez and dupatta, cringed a bit from the full-frontal image the mirror reflected, but decided I just had to try out this dress, even if I never dared to purchase it. You know what they say about life: it just takes a few seconds for your life to change. My life changed the moment I pulled the sleeveless number over my head and saw the years peel back and fall on that fitting-room floor. Gone was the middle-aged, rather frumpy, lumpy person I saw myself as, and in her place stood a confident, elegant woman who was significantly lighter and seemed to own the room.

Now, this might seem strange and bizarre to a lot of people but back when I was in my teens, growing up in a small suburban town outside Mumbai, only 'forward' girls wore anything other than a churidar-kurta. Jeans and lipstick were for 'forward' girls and only God could save them from the self-righteous *mavshi*s in the neighbourhood who kept a hawk's eye out to make sure these fast numbers did not so much as look at their sons, let alone talk to them. The most fashion forward I dared to go, for the longest time, was to get myself one of those tight, figure-hugging Sadhana-type churidars that made it a struggle to scramble onto and off the local train to my college. When I was eighteen I mustered the courage and, having made my mother my co-conspirator, bought myself a pair of jeans and a camouflage shirt which was most happening in those days. I felt like Zeenat Aman that day and had to tear myself away from college because, for the first time ever, I felt glamorous but when I got back home Achan saw me in my new threads and did not speak to me for a week. And he was one of the most progressive men I have ever known but such were the social mores of the middle-class town we lived in.

My rendezvous with the little blue dress marks the beginning of an ongoing affair. Give me the slightest chance and I am ready to pull out my teeny-weeny clothes (OK, I might be exaggerating here; they merely stop at my knees) and go kill them. Not that I go out that much but when the burdens of the world seem too much to carry, or when all I have done through the day is stare at a blank screen with words refusing to come out of my jaded brain, I do pull out a lovely little dress, wear my red wedge heels, and admire myself. I walk around the house, try to take a couple of selfies, send them to my sisters in other corners of the world, and when they have admired me I go back to my desk and just bring out some smashing pages.

Cut to the present and the dialogue in my head goes like this: 'Shall I wear the black sleeveless dress? Fits beautifully. But *Vogue* said the other day that wearing black during the day ages mature women and accentuates their fine lines. Ditch it. Will the lime-green linen shift dress work? Yes, I love it. But wait, I don't have footwear to go with it since the daughter snitched my wedges a while back.

Ditto with yellow, pink, and navy blue dresses. It will just have to be the burnt-orange dress. Works well with my dusky (read pigmented) skin and I can manage the red wedges with it. Plus, I have a great leather bag to complete the ensemble. Passing thought: *maybe the fashion police have a point when they say that a pair of shoes of every colour is a MUST-HAVE in every woman's wardrobe.'*

Thursday morning. Hours of paroxysm as I plan the day and I am wondering if the spouse disappeared to work in unholy hurry to escape the usual trap which goes like this:

Me: 'Should I wear this dress? Or this one?'

Spouse: 'The beige looks nice.'

Me: 'You are so boring. You always want me to wear beige. I hate beige. I know what it is. You want me to look frumpy. The other day I wore red lipstick and you said it was too dark. Do you know the whole world is wearing red lipstick? I'm the only one with a husband who is always trying to keep me from looking good. You just don't appreciate me!'

The moment I mentioned the impending lunch last night, the spouse had pretended to check his email and let me know, very casually, of course, that he needed to leave for work by 8 a.m.

Not that I'm complaining. When I have to go out these days, I like some space to myself. I like to try out what I'm wearing and that usually means trying out six different dresses and opting for a random seventh, by when I am sweating and want another shower. Then there is the make-up.

If you are about my age you will know what I mean by the perils of trying to put on some eyeliner. There was a time when it was easy. You just took out the little black bottle, looked in the mirror, and drew your eyeliner over. Within seconds you had smouldering dark eyes, ready to bewitch all and sundry.

It is different these days. You take out the eyeliner and totter in your heels towards the dressing table or the bathroom mirror and realize that you can't see a thing!

'Shit, I've gone blind. Err no, I have forgotten my specs.' Frantic search for specs and after finding it inside the fridge where I left them when I went to get sliced cucumber to put on the eyes to nix the puffiness and get them party-ready, I'm back at the mirror, hands trembling like an alcoholic in the throes of withdrawal. 'Shit, shit! How the heck can I use my eyeliner when I have specs over my eyes?' The end result of the struggle with the eyeliner is that I look like someone has given me a black eye.

Quick rush to take it all off with non-alcohol-based make-up remover and repeat steps mentioned above. Too much trouble, you think? The other day I almost fell off the chair when I read a prominent women's lifestyle magazine going on happily about cutting strips of Scotch tape and putting it on the eyelids before drawing various lines and triangles all over, just so that the poor woman doing it could nail the 'winged eyes' which is all the rage just now. Not being able to see enough to cut pieces of Scotch tape from the damn roll, I have given up hopes of getting *that* look. For now, the repaired black-eye look is what I manage with.

But I am jumping the gun. What about prepping before the make-up? There was a time when, if you had to go hang out with friends or shop or lunch, all you needed was to apply the family's favourite talcum powder, kept neatly in Amma's plastic container with a powder puff. You opened the round plastic container, ran the puff over the face, and rushed off wherever you were headed. In the early years of my marriage, I took to shaking powder from the bottle straight onto my hands, rubbing my palms together, and then rubbing the powder onto the face before picking up the wailing toddler to be dropped off at playschool and heading to whichever press conference I had to cover.

That was my familiarity with make-up until I was almost forty when, on a visit to the US of A, I dragged the unsuspecting spouse to the flagship store of a prominent make-up brand, where a very cool sales executive looked at my face and said, 'Dahling, you look like you have cement on your face.' That visit ended with me carrying a hundred dollars worth of cosmetics out of the store and it left my husband ashen and shaken to the core. It was 2008 and a hundred dollars on cosmetics was like taking him to the cleaners. We crossed the road from the brand store to Central Park where he lay quietly panting on a carpet of burnt ochre and red leaves, under a brilliant blue autumn sky. He said he was tired from the walking but, in retrospect, I think he was shaken from the enormity of the damage to his wallet. I vividly remember the colour of the leaves on which we lay; it was the same shade of the lipstick that I had purchased at the store and almost cost me my marriage. Not that he said anything to me. Only that I looked brilliant with the makeover they had given me, but I did notice that he stopped having his favourite cappuccino at Starbucks for an entire month after my outing to the cosmetics store in NYC.

So here is what I learnt at the cosmetics store all those years ago. It is not enough to just have the face you are born with. Once you have grown enough to know what is good for you, it is important to use cosmetics to sculpt and chisel your face. Use the entire arsenal the industry has created for you: brushes, sponges, combs, and such other things to create an illusion around your face. Then there is the stuff that promises you perfection straight out of a bottle but doesn't tell you the fine print.

So, there you are, lazing on the sofa in your PJs, when you get a call and the voice at the other end is inviting you to the most exclusive do of the month. And it is two hours from now.

You rush into the shower, rush out to get into a dress after discarding five others and then:

Step 1: Project make-up. Take out what seems like a trunk full of stuff and line them up on the dressing table. Begin with a face-lifting moisturizer and apply in deft upward strokes. Wait for five minutes before you apply primer in three versions, one each for the face, lips, and eyes, and let that settle on the skin. For the uninitiated, primers are great products that smoothen the skin and allow the rest of the cosmetics to glide over smoothly and prevent them from settling in the fine lines or frown lines to make you look like a bad-tempered witch.

Step 2: Take out the very expensive, very small jar of concealer and dot it under your eyes and age spots, if you have any. Blend deftly with concealer brush or sponge. Well, I would if I could find them. The sponge, not the under-eye circles or age spots, both of which I have in plenty. As usual, having misplaced said sponge, I use the corner of my face towel to apply primer and glance up to see I am now looking like a clown escaped from the circus.

Step 3: Bring out the very expensive, very small jar of light diffusing foundation that glides on like silk onto skin and makes you look like an ethereal being. Being convinced by the sales executive at the store that I needed foundation with yellow undertones, I glance into the mirror to see I now look like I am suffering from a bad case of jaundice.

Step 4: The blusher. The apple of my cheek has disappeared. I used to have one but once I hit my late forties the apple seems to have disintegrated and all I have in its place is a forlorn expression. So I grin as widely as I can and imagining that said apple is at a specific position, I apply the blusher just under it. My transformation into a clown is almost complete. A clown who is also blushing like a bashful bride.

Step 5: Putting on lipstick should be the easiest thing ever: pull off the lid, apply lipstick on lips, and that's it. But no. That was back in the 1970s and 1980s. The procurement and application of lipstick is a complex game that involves much brain work and patience. You go to the mall and wander around in the cosmetics section, which is like a maze you can't get out of and at each counter the girls will show you glittering, dazzling collections of lipsticks that promise to make your thin lips plump or the other way around. Then there are creamy lipsticks and matte ones; there are high-definition ones, and ones in liquid form. There are lip stains and the last time I checked there were also crayons. (And I thought crayons were what we used to draw people with stick-like arms and legs back in third grade.) Applying lipstick is now an art that involves spending large amounts of your hard-earned moolah. At anything between a thousand to three thousand rupees a piece, buying lipstick induces a month's worth of guilt in me and, add the cost of that lip pencil to give definition to your lips and it socks the wallet a hard one. My friendly salon lady taught me the art of using a lip pencil to draw a perfect bow-shaped lip and that, I am told, is the perfect way to zap my thinning lips – yes, in addition to thinning hair, the fifties also marks the thinning of your once gloriously plump lips and the mysterious disappearance of your apple cheeks.

I know I'm in danger of being labelled a vain or insecure fifty-year-old but I am all for whatever makes me feel good about myself, and if bow-shaped lips does it for me I'm going for it. Remember how the actor Rekha disappeared for a few months to the US some decades ago and emerged all svelte and diva-like? She apparently worked out her body, did lots of yoga, and learnt the art of applying make-up from a pro; the new, improved Rekhaji had the industry eating out of her hands and chasing after her with roles that her rivals would give an arm and a leg for. If Rekhaji can do it, why not poor old me?

Coming back to the lunch date, though, I'm all set with make-up and the glamorous dress and am just admiring myself one last time in the mirror when I notice it: the nasty silver glint on my chin that has recently driven me crazy. The fifties are also when you first sprout hair in all sorts of unexpected places, including your chin. White ones. When I was in school I used to watch in horror as my grandma and her spinster sisters absentmindedly pulled at their chin hair. The other day I was watching television when the fledgling slapped away my hand from my face. 'Mom, you are constantly pulling your chin hair. Either get it waxed or stop pulling on it in public. You look weird.'

Serves me right for sneering at my grandma and her sisters. What went around has come around and how – I have white hair on my eyebrows too! But you can't keep a smart woman down with these tiny setbacks. I have found my weapon of mass destruction for chin hair. On Amazon. An innocent-looking spring with florescent pink handles that I simply roll on my chin to pull out every hair there is. Ta-da! Evenings at the household are now spent in companionable silence with the spouse snoozing in front of the telly and yours truly eliminating the enemy on the chin with the new-found companion, the 'facial epilator stick', which, incidentally, has also been gifted to the sisters and the mother.

Happiness is to be shared, right?

HOT MAMA!

THERE ARE HOT MAMAS and Hotter Mamas and then there is me. I'm way hotter than any Hot Mamas out there and I can prove it to you.

Every morning, afternoon, or evening as I sit quaffing tea or eating a cupcake or something equally fattening that puts me in sugar heaven, I set eyes upon half a dozen Hot Mamas in my apartment block doing what they do best: being Hot Mamas. It is not easy being a Hot Mama. In fact, I have a sneaking admiration for them considering how hard they have to work to keep their Hot Mama crowns.

For instance, the first thing you need to have to be a Hot Mama is determination. Loads of it. You have to be determined to get the butt off the sofa where you are binge-watching something or the other on telly. Such as the serial in which a woman, actually a snake in disguise, is trying to make out with the husband who is not a snake and is trying to not make out with her because he does not want a snake-child in human disguise.

A Hot Mama must firmly put away the temptation of watching the intrigue-filled making-out session and the temptation of falling asleep on the couch and go hunt for suitable gym apparel, which, in itself, is probably harder than Vasco da Gama's voyage to India. To begin with, gym clothing is not what it used to be back in the early part of this century when I Iast least pretended to go to the gym and work out. Back then the most adventurous you could get with workout gear was ditching the black track pants and tee for blue, pink, or red ones. Also, the really adventurous girls got themselves sleeveless tees. And wore headbands to hold their hair in place as they huffed and puffed.

Not anymore. Shopping for gym wear is way more complicated now and includes making conversation with the sales guys who distract unsuspecting women with their rippling muscles and jeans ripped dangerously close to unmentionable places. These guys will walk you down bewildering mazes of trainers, runners, jogging shoes, some with mesh to allow your feet to breathe, some with bounce, some with memory, and some lightweight. There is a delicious irony to it, and if I ever decide to hit the gym I will opt for the shoe with memory foam, even though my own memory has hot-footed it out of my head. I will also check out the yoga-mat shoes because I like the idea of yoga and the idea of snoozing off on the mat once I have finished with it.

Somehow, though, I don't think the manufacturer meant for the shoe buyer to be thinking of sleep in connection with their workout shoes.

The shops that sell workout gear are no longer shops; they are gargantuan caves full of glamorous, glitzy wares that draw you deeper and deeper into their innards, where fashionably thin women are checking out brands that sell teeny-weeny cycling shorts, even tinier bralets and crystal-embedded workout shorts that I would hate to waste inside a gym. Those shorts positively shout for attention and I would hate to waste their attention-grabbing potential at the gym where most souls are so smitten with themselves they are hardly likely to notice somebody else's butt, even if they are flashing crystals. I would wear them to a party, if I could manage to fit into one of these. And if somebody were to invite me to a party, of course.

Talking about parties, the latest trend amongst the bold and the beautiful is to host these frighteningly glamorous parties where everybody wears gym wear designed to show off their worked-out bods, glistening biceps, worked-out abs and glutes, and their chiselled booties. Nobody gets to eat cheese-loaded nachos or fries at these parties, nor drown in alcohol. The beautiful people at gym parties sip on green smoothies with spinach, avocado, micro-greens, Brussels sprouts, and the conversation revolves around the latest workout trend. And while they are so conversing, they snack on delicate, nutrition-laden bites of roasted quinoa or millet or something equally nasty. There is a reason I am not into gyms and gym parties. The last time I went to an all-girls party, we all sat around a table creaking with goodies: nachos with cheese, samosas, potato wafers, fried cheese balls, and endless rounds of vodka. There was not a healthy snack or smoothie for miles around and everything went off smoothly. Some of us ended the night sliding off the chairs and snoozing under the table and, no, we did not need yoga mats for it.

Being a Hot Mama calls for other sacrifices, too, and largely it is the family that pays the price so that the Mama gets to retain her figure. The neighbourhood grocer who delivers weekly groceries to our apartment complex recently added me to a WhatsApp group where everybody lists their grocery requirements. I am astounded at what families are now eating: rotis with oats added to wheat flour, with some soya flour added for good measure. The other day one of the Hot Mamas asked for a mixture of tapioca and potato starch, banana flour, cashew milk and a few other equally baffling things to bake a cake for her daughter's birthday! In the interest of peace in the neighbourhood I reserved comment on the cake. In the good old days birthday cakes were deliciously decadent with chocolate chips and came with toasted marshmallows and enough chocolate icing to keep everyone on a sugar high for a week.

As for me, after what seems like an eternity of eating oats for breakfast while the rest of the family hogs idli, dosa, puri and fat cheese toasts, I have, finally, been cured of the habit. 'There is nothing that a plateful of rice and sambar can't fix. Also, you need to eat more coconut in your food. I am seventy and have eaten sambar and coconut chutney all my life,' is my Malayali matriarch's battle hymn. For years she has been nagging me into eating these things and I, being as mulish as her, have insisted that my eating habits are my business and I am not going to trade my oats for her breakfast choice. 'Eat idli. Oats are for horses, not for people,' she would say, daring me with the gleam in her eye to take her on.

A few months ago when I was cooking oats for breakfast, the thought came to me from the universe that I could not bear to eat another spoon of oats in my life, not even if it was to be smothered in a dozen gulab jamuns. I walked over to the fridge, took out the dosa batter for Hassled Harry's breakfast, and tucked into six ghee-laden dosas. Never felt as good as I did in that moment. The matriarch is always right but my pride won't allow me to admit this to her.

But coming back to the Hot Mamas in my apartment complex, they are a hard-working lot. Every morning, when I sit reading the newspaper at my usual perch in my balcony, I catch sight of the motley group huffing and puffing so that they can somehow get into the coveted little black dress after nearly driving themselves to death with three hundred squats, running up and down the complex with weights on their legs or backpacks full of dead weight. Some days they play basketball under the blazing summer sun and some days they walk on all fours doggie-style or do rabbit jumps (remember them from PT class in school?). They have a female trainerzilla (my word) to crack the whip on them and I have, on occasion, wondered how it would be to live with someone whose favourite words are, 'One more time! Get your tail up, come on now, let us do it fast and furious!'

The ladies have their rewards for doing it fast and furious all week long. They get 'cheat days' when they can have a tiny slice of chocolate cake or an ice cream and two spoonfuls of rice with their dal. Still no fried aloo or pappadam with their meals but at least they get to have chocolate. And they get the pleasure of going out on their monthly 'workout girls' party' where they get to burn the dance floor in little black dresses, flaunting their glutes, abs and all the rest of their worked-out gorgeousness.

As for me, I don't need to work that hard to be a Hot Mama. One minute I am eating chocolate ice cream and the next minute I am swimming in a pool of my own sweat. On the wrong side of fifty, our hot flushes make us Hot Babes just like that.

THE PURSUIT OF MIDDLE-AGED SEXINESS

I WAS AT LUNCH with the girl gang sometime before I turned fifty and the conversation veered towards how we were ageing and what we would do in our fifties. This particularly deep discussion came after one of the girls, who is on a mission to 'go white', turned up looking like a goddess in a loose, flowing summer gown that took the temperature inside the restaurant a few notches up.

Not all of us agreed that she needed to stop colouring her hair. 'You are only sixty. It is too early to stop colouring,' one of the girls said. 'Do it after you have grandchildren,' another said and soon the topic evolved into the usual 'how to be fabulous at fifty' sort of conversation.

The subject of this discussion suddenly stood up and said, 'Girls, sexy is as sexy does. I feel sexy with white hair. I think this is the most beautiful I have felt in a long time.'

It was around the same time that I also read a book that was all about how forty-plus women need not throw in their hats but can actually transform themselves into these glamorous babes with smoky eyes, sexy clothes, and come-hither painted nails. I have had that book on my mind for the longest time and have made several false starts to getting to be the sexy babe in it. The trouble is, unlike my friend who has found nirvana in her white hair, I'm still searching for mine in malls and stores that stock clothes designed to make every woman look like a diva. Except me, of course. I'm still sitting on the fence about the clothes that are being designed for women today, especially those with the generous curves and the love handles that come along when you hit the mid-forties.

A few months ago, the fledgling, who has been witness to my fashion blues, said to me, 'Why don't you just go to the mall one day? And go alone. Take your time to try things on and don't ask the store staff and your besties for their opinion.'

With that in mind I visited the neighbourhood mall, determined to return with enough gorgeous, glamorous new clothes to get me out of my frumpy-clothes-induced blue funk. First stop was a happening Spanish label that my twenty-six-year old frequents, with collateral damage to my bank balance. She looks like a million bucks in the brand's clothing, though, and so, like a homing pigeon, I headed towards the store which had SALE emblazoned outside. Whoever said the zero-sized model is passé should check out this store. I searched high and low, pulled out dozens of things lying in bargain boxes and even looked under the table where stuff seemed to have been discarded, but there was nary a piece of clothing to hide my generous, curvaceous assets. Not unless I wanted to outfit myself in prison-uniform striped PJs and oversized shirts to go with them. And that would do nothing for the middle-aged babe that I wanted to be. Besides, I suspected this would drive the spouse out of the bedroom, fearful of my PMS, and I would not blame him.

Ever tried getting into one of those fashionably thin, dangerously low pants that come in the cutest colours? I had to fairly tie myself in knots and consider lying on the trial-room floor to wriggle myself into one, only to be sorely disappointed. Unless I wanted to wear them on my knee, I would have to abandon this fashion trend because the damned things hit a solid roadblock at the thighs.

My Mission Glam has led me up other sartorial paths – with dismal results – in the last couple of years. For instance, a few months ago I noticed a sudden spike in the number of drop-dead glamorous women sporting tops and dresses with what seemed like holes on the sleeves, at the exact point where shoulder joints end and the arms begin. Upon casually mentioning this to the fledgling I was told that this was a new fashion trend and not a hole in the sleeve. 'They are cold shoulders, Mom!' I was told with the customary eye roll. In my youth a cold shoulder meant other things: it meant snubbing someone. You never wanted to be at the receiving end of a cold shoulder but these days if you get yourself a cold shoulder you will be one amongst the fashion-forward folks.

Ever tried ripped jeans? I was in London last year when ripped jeans were absolutely the thing to flaunt and having seen them on hoardings and in every self-respecting store from Zara, Debenhams and M&S to Primark, I decided I would buy myself a pair. I got my prized possession home having burnt up a cool packet on it and was more than hot under the collar when the mother, who sat on a rocking chair, eating fries, looked me up and down the next morning on my way out and said, 'You need a fresh pair of jeans. You can't be a famous author and roam around in torn jeans. Somebody might think you are hard up.' I fled upstairs to get out of my ripped jeans and soon exchanged them for a pair of 'boyfriend' jeans instead, though it mystifies me why people have named women's apparel after men, especially because we all know lots of men who think jeans are things you don't have to wash. Ever. Eeeks.

Much as I am a fan of all things trendy, there are days when I wish I was back in a time when things were simpler. In the mid-1980s, when I was stepping into my twenties and starting to wear sarees, things were simpler, or, at least, they were simpler in the Bombay suburb I grew up in. The mother took you to the tailor and got you two blouses: a black and a white. They had high necks and the sleeve length ended at the elbows. You borrowed the saree and even the petticoats – white, black, and maybe a green and a red – from the mother.

Things are different today. My mother almost fell off her armchair the other day when I opened a courier package and out fell a mermaid-shaped lycra petticoat with *love handle control features and a padded rear side.* I almost died of shock, too, because I had no clue that shopping online for a petticoat would bring home this all-new contraption parading as the humble petticoat.

Have you noticed how good tailors are becoming an endangered species? Turns out most of them prefer to work in air-conditioned malls instead of working for a pittance in their own trade. And the few tailors that are left have been taken over by so-called designers who use the phenomenal skills of said tailors to make big bucks for themselves with the result that a blouse that should cost five hundred rupees to stitch now costs between two and five thousand. I know of one corporate maven who shells out over seven thousand rupees for every blouse she gets tailored!

I was trying to get myself a few blouses made recently because I have eaten myself out of my old ones; the entire exercise left me weak-kneed and quivering with anxiety with the number of decisions I had to make. I could make blouses with a princess cut, empire sleeves, or bell sleeves; blouses can be combined with net, lace, sequins, semi-precious stones, and peek-a-boo design features that can leave the beholder giddy. Meanwhile, I am nursing a frozen shoulder from trying to pull down the zip at the side of blouses, or, worse, zips on the back. My domestic help had to rescue me the other day after I tied myself up in a knot trying to reach my back to pull the zip down on my fancy new blouse. With these new blouses you don't have to worry about wearing a bra because they come with bra cups. My problem is there has been no cup made that can hold my considerable rogue assets, and, so, I have to make new-fangled blouses that will still allow me to wear the good old bra. The spouse is convinced I have lost it in the quest for my Inner Diva. As for me, I am hoping that the old blouses with front buttons make a comeback.

And while we are at it, can we have bras with front hooks, too, please, *please*? It is way too much trouble and too much struggle each day to get to the damn hook every morning. It is coming to a stage when I am wishing we have a new braless trend here in India. If Hollywood babes can do it, why can't we?

As for me, having flirted with daring scooped backs that displayed the ample tyres on my rear side and a kaftan dress that made me resemble a penguin in a flap, I have found peace in the size XL of an Indian brand that makes clever dresses for real women like me. Ah, bliss!

And oh, did I tell you the near orgasmic pleasure of gorging on an almond muffin and a slice of heavenly banana loaf at the cafe on my way out of the mall? Never mind the middle-aged babe. I will make do with the middle-aged part. And that shiny glazed doughnut at that cafe.

MY KIND OF VACATION

I HATE VACATIONS. I truly do. The kind of vacations where I must wake up at the crack of dawn and gad about until my legs are about to fall off and my head feels like a hundred people are hammering away on the inside.

Vacations where tour companies conspire to rule my life are definitely not for me. Breakfast at 7 a.m. (!!) Board bus at 7:30 a.m. Tourist sights A, B, C, D, E, F until 1:30 p.m. Lunch by 2 p.m. and tourist sights I, J, K, L, F until 7:30 p.m., with a weak tea-bag tea at a crowded cafe at a petrol station thrown in between. The torture does not end there. Dance and entertainment from 8 p.m. to 9:30 p.m. Dinner by 10:30 p.m.

The only entertainment that I can imagine after the torture of the entire day would be if someone gave me carte blanche to take a whip to the enthusiastic tour guide and chase him away with a stern warning to not show up the next morning. As for dinner and barbecue, I have had so much of the enthusiastic bunch during the day on the tourist bus that I am ready to throw up at the prospect of sharing any more face time with them. Would rather pop a pill and go to bed and dream of taking the busload of merrymakers to a distant location and, somehow, losing them there and winning myself some quiet time.

When it comes to vacations I have a bad name in the family because they happen to be beach lovers who want to soak up the sun, frolic in the sea, go off on those vertigo-inducing speedboats, and do everything they can possibly think up to put life and limb at risk. The last time I went to the beach in Goa there were about three thousand beach bums, most of them on their worst behaviour, trying hard to look cool roaming around with beer bottles and gawking at honeymooning couples engaged in some hardcore PDA. By the way, what is with the arms full of bangles, stilettos and gowns on a beach? I once saw a woman in this get-up trying to get on a water scooter and the spectacle provided much entertainment to those gathered there. The lovelorn husband did not quite know how to deal with his damsel's distress but she somehow managed to clamber on and I was glad to see her grit and determination: have gown, will wear, even if it is on the beach and while clambering onto a water scooter. Girls like these give hope to my cynical soul but I would not dare try the same stunt myself.

Vacations used to be fun while I was in my twenties and thirties and there were no cell phones and no social media and, so, everybody could go off to vacation without the burden of looking good enough to eat while actually not eating anything so that you look good on the Insta post. I was recently looking at pictures of a twenty-year-old me on vacation with my extended family and the sight warmed the cockles of my heart. I was in a billowing maroon skirt and a black tee, my hair a glorious mess and face toasted brown so that only the eyes shone bright and happy. There was not a selfie pout in that frame and the picture looked much the better for it.

Vacations today are much more complex, and the very word puts the fear of God into me because I know it will entail much searching online by the techie husband – at least two months of searching – who says it is so because I am fussy about vacations! We once went for a two-week-long vacation to Sikkim and spent the first week sleeping because we were so tired from the midnight hours spent searching for vacation destinations. Plus, when we got there we found there were more potholes than roads leading up to the wonderful place, and seven hours on a potholed road is a bad start to any vacation.

Vacations today also entail much hard work and that pretty much destroys the joy of embarking on one. For instance, have you seen how the glossies devote page upon page to the resort-wear collection of one or the other designer? The women in the pages have marvellously toned bodies and are either seen gazing at the sunset from under beautiful gazebos or emerging from the pool or sea in jaw-dropping swimwear and trendier cover-ups. My grouse with resort-wear designers is that their creations are far too expensive for broke authors. Besides, the way these clothes are designed leaves far too little to the imagination and my imagination boggles at the thought of imposing the sight of my dimpled thighs on unsuspecting folk chilling by the poolside.

My Libran nature kicks in hard when I pack for my vacations. Should I follow the husband's strategy and simply pack two pairs of jeans and four T-shirts, or should I follow my own instinct and, therefore, pack the following: two pairs of jeans, six tees, three glamorous evening outfits for romantic dinners, four lipsticks, four pairs of footwear, two for day, two for night. Plus, I like to carry my own bath towel. I no longer carry any sexy lingerie since Hassled Harry and I are now firmly in the friend zone. Which should also automatically teach me to drop the three glamorous evening outfits for our romantic dinner rendezvous but I am still living in hope. The last time we went on a vacation I carried my own bedsheet too because I read somewhere that duvets in hotel rooms are among the most infected and dirty things you can think of.

I hate to admit this but my idea of a vacation is to make it to some luxury hotel – I don't care where it is, as long as they have the best bed, a great view, luxury toiletries, and a bathtub where I can soak away, while sipping on some bubbly. The icing on the cake is when the spouse decides he wants to go to the spa and I get to hog the bed the entire afternoon.

I love these hotel rooms for any number of reasons but the top two would be that I don't have to do the dusting or attend to the doorbell, and hotels spoil guests rotten with decadent chocolates and other freebies and did I mention they have the best toiletries? The last time I checked into one of these hotels while on work, they had an Indian brand of toiletries which I had been lusting after for a long time but never mustered the courage to buy, thanks to the price tag. I lost no time slathering on their all-natural moisturizers till I became as slippery as an eel and went to sleep with the aroma of organic de-stressing, sleep-enhancing spray on my pillow. Needless to say, the toiletries came home safely tucked in my suitcase and I am saving them for when I need some pampering.

While on the topic of toiletries I worry sometimes about guest etiquette when faced with temptation in the form of toiletries offered by hotel chains. Are these for use only in the hotel room and to be discarded afterwards? Considering the hard-earned money I spend to check into these hotels, I am of the opinion I can carry some of it back home. Only toiletries though. Not bathrobes and slippers and certainly not the goose-feather pillows. But the tempting little bottles of lotions and potions can be yours guiltlessly. And so, I have merrily helped myself to a couple of jars of moisturizers, small bars of soap, and shower caps till a friend in the hospitality business mentioned how hotels are so intent on delivering guest satisfaction that they now know almost everything about them. Everything. The housekeeping staff, I'm told, are the ones who report on the guest's propensity to this or the other brand of toiletries and many, many other things. You get the drift, from the stuff we discard in waste bins... But did you think this has stopped me from taking my supply of shower caps and lotions from my hotel stays? Certainly not. I have a moment of self-doubt but I firmly push it away and go home happily, my booty safe in my bag, to be arranged in a row in my bathroom cabinet. This is one of the things that I certainly like about my vacations.

Another thing I like about being on vacation is that, for once, I am not in charge of putting food on the table. Not that I have cooked in many years but I still do have to exercise my brains to let the cook know what to procure and prepare for the family. I love the fact that my hotel stay allows me the luxury of waking up late and going down to the restaurant to a king's breakfast. Doughnuts for breakfast! I'm like a child in a toy store when I am at the breakfast buffet. Besides doughnuts, I also help myself to croissants, Danish pastries, a muffin, a glass of juice, two cups of masala chai, and, then, to assuage my guilt, I also eat a bowl of muesli with some healthy nuts and seeds. At home I eat a bowl of oats and fruit. Every single day.

I would not mind moving permanently to live in a hotel room. I don't have to make the beds, I can watch endless TV, I get to use heavenly toiletries and I get to eat THE BREAKFAST. Beats the hell out of living in your own home. The problem is the spouse and the kid might want to move in with me and that defeats the very purpose. I might have to share my bathroom. And I never, ever do that.

EVERYTHING OLD IS CHIC AGAIN – WELL, ALMOST

EVERYTHING OLD IS COOL and trendy suddenly. Can I please go back to the 1900s?

I have a friend who has enough moolah to buy the best things from the most expensive stores in the country; instead, she wanders around the lanes and by-lanes of Juna Bazaar in Maximum City, trawling its hole-in-the-wall shops for things old and forgotten. I have been with her on a couple of such missions and have wondered at her keen sense of spotting the diamond in the rough, figuratively speaking, of course.

From all her poking around in old shops and establishments she has struck pay dirt in the form of a dozen pure silver, monogrammed dessert spoons from the 1930s, a solid silver frame for a clutch purse (which she transformed into a vintage clutch with raw silk), pearls and semi-precious stones, and a vegetable chopper of German make of God-alone-knows what vintage but is the best veggie chopper I have seen in the business. And, oh, not to forget an antique door handle in the shape of a preening parrot, which now adorns her front door. As for me, when I accompany her on these missions, I mostly hold my breath to avoid the mustiness and wait to exhale, which is mostly two hours later.

This selfsame friend is also a shopper for everything old in jewellery, be it junk jewellery to wear with a retro-inspired dress or expensive baubles that can no longer be purchased new because the master karigars who made these are long dead and their children prefer working in malls as security staff to hunching over a single piece of jewellery for days together, for a few hundred rupees. My friend and I occasionally drop in at a jeweller's store; she's as sharp a Shylock as you can imagine, who goes weak in the knees at the mere mention of old and antique.

When the twain do meet, there is no scope of ever getting a word in sideways because the air is thick with 'oohs' and 'aaahs' as they exclaim over what was once a gleaming gold saree border, now faded and frayed but still beautiful, which he had acquired from a kabadiwallah who bought a cartload of stuff from a geriatric Parsi lady for a couple of thousand rupees. The kabadiwallah's acquisitions also include a bridal gaara, now falling to bits, from which he has cut out the intricate pearl-embroidered border, which will now be sold to an 'old-struck' young woman for a hell of a lot of money.

When it comes to all things old, what is food for one is probably poison for another. A friend of mine once told me about her mother, who, upon the friend's grandfather's death, decided to give away his belongings to the family cook, a portly old fellow who had loyally looked after the old man. The old grouch, also nudging his mid-sixties, grumbled at the stinginess of the household when the lady of the house gave him the old man's ancient wristwatch and rued his luck that he had spent his life working for such selfish people. When she heard her mother had disposed of her grandfather's wristwatch, my friend was struck dumb; turns out what the mother mistook for a worthless old watch was actually a vintage Rolex. And when the mother refused to ask for the old watch back from the family retainer, it was up to my friend to procure a gleaming new watch and gift it to the beaming cook who was more than happy to part with the worthless old watch. 'Your mother is really a very stingy woman. Don't tell her I said this,' the old man said to my friend, unable to take his eyes off his windfall.

In her early thirties my mother, then already a mother to three daughters and a son, pined away for all the things her husband could not buy her. She hated the fact that she could not have a sofa, a showcase, and a two-in-one music player because there was never any money left after paying the bills. One evening we came home from school to see her beaming from ear to ear. She had palmed off the 'old, rickety, ugly' Murphy LP player to the kabadiwallah and got him to shell out three hundred and fifty rupees for it. As for us kids, we got to eat samosas and bhel from the chaatwallah around the corner that evening and she got herself a new saree. (Although, I still feel the occasional pang when I think of the fabulous time we kids used to have listening to Rafi and Asha belt out fast numbers on the record player.)

Collecting old things comes with its own set of heartaches. I came home a few years ago to find two dazzling yellow brass floor lamps in place of the burnished gold antique ones for which I had forked out a big portion of my then modest monthly salary. Turns out that I had forgotten that Diwali was nearing, and my domestic help had used generous amounts of some gooey-stuff-in-a-bottle to polish my lamps so that they would shine bright and earn her the fat bonus she takes home every year. While she was at it, she also polished all the antique door handles in the house – the ones that I spent days scouring Juna Bazaar to acquire – and the effect was so blinding the family almost considered wearing glares inside the house.

On the other hand, if everything old is chic again, how come most people, especially retailers, treat me like the plague?

The other day I was in the mall killing time as I waited for a friend to arrive for us to grab some coffee and share some goss. I wandered into one of those large brand shops that sell everything from false boobs to eyelashes, and all in between.

Since I am more often than not on a mission these days to become Red Hot Mama, I made a beeline for the cosmetics section where three or four salesgirls sat around languidly painting their lips fire-engine red and putting on mascara to elongate their eyelashes enough to give serious competition to Rapunzel's locks. None of them noticed me for the next ten minutes when I tested every one of their red lipsticks on the inside of my wrist. It was only when I noisily cleared my throat and came close to stomping my feet like a spoilt brat that one of the girls looked up from her task of painting her nails. 'Can you show me some red lipsticks please?' I asked, breathless with anticipation, adroitly sidestepping the horrified look she aimed at me.

Suffice it to say the red lipstick search did not do much for my morale. After showing me a few shades of red, all of them wishy-washy and apologetic, she said to me, 'Ma'am, why don't you look for some browns and nudes? *Aapke age ke laydiz brown lipstick lagaate hain*. Ma'am, can I show you some skin-firming, line-minimizing creams? Those are our bestselling items for women of your age.'

'Certainly not,' I said, tottering off to drown my sorrow in a cup of ginger tea and some toast, and ponder about all things old that are now as good as gold. Except human beings, of course.

If everything old is fashionable and sought after, why am I – and others like me who are on the wrong side of fifty – not needed anymore? I know everything has an expiry date, but we don't carry 'best before' dates on our lined foreheads, do we? Why is it that youngsters, even my own fledgling, go silent, when I enter their room, until then full of raucous laughter? On the other hand, I much prefer the silence to the smirks or eye rolls that sometimes welcome a group of us fifty-somethings when we enter a coffee shop or pub populated by eighteen-somethings.

There are other reasons I like the old and the beautiful. The familiarity of names of things, for example. In the olden days a pin was a tiny steel contraption that you used when the buttons on your shirt front popped. They were available for five rupees a dozen and there were plenty of them in every woman's purse, to be pulled out in the event of a wardrobe malfunction. The pins also had other handy uses, such as stringing your PJs and petticoats and holding the saree pleats in place.

These days 'pins' are a combination of numbers that you must remember if you want to purchase a dress, a toothpaste, or a diamond ring – not that I could afford a diamond ring, pin or no pin. At airports and cinema halls, at malls and at the ATM, the number of people who have seen me pulling my hair because I have forgotten my PIN is now legion. Why the heck should I have to remember a PIN to use my hard-earned money to buy me some dessert? Or shoes?

Then there is the cloud. When we were growing up, clouds were in the sky and sometimes they were white and cottony, and danced in the sky on bright, clear days. And during the rains they were grey, morose, and puffed-up like a giant grey cotton candy that spewed rain. These days a cloud is where you can store everything: zillions of pictures, documents, PPT presentations – in short, you can back up your life on a cloud. I'm worried. What if this new-age cloud bursts one day? Would that mean that all your life secrets will be spewed wide in the open for all and sundry to laugh at? Just asking.

The old times were innocent times, things were less complicated. For instance, you could hold hands with your best female friend and roam around the entire afternoon and nobody would look at you strangely. Contrast it with the current times – I was travelling through the US of A last year and remember having been at the receiving end of several stares because my daughter and I would roam around with fingers intertwined, in malls, gardens, and high streets. I did not realize till a friend told me that we were probably mistaken for a same-sex couple!

In the old times you could hug and even pull the cheeks of a random cute baby you met while walking in the park. Not anymore. The world is likely to label you either an evil kidnapper or a perv stalking kids. So, don't hug a baby. Unless it is yours. The brave new world will frown at your bizarre behaviour.

In the old times there was Cutex and red was everybody's favourite nail polish colour. Getting your nails polished these days is an exercise that merits going to business school. You get to choose between long-lasting or quick-drying nail polish and you have to pick from matte, pearl, shimmer, glitter, high-shine, and growth-enhancing polishes. As if that is not enough decision to make, you also have to choose between an ordinary polish job or gel nails. I would chew my nails right off my fingers if I had to make so many decisions in the old days. These days you can't even chew your nails because they are now gel-encrusted aliens that don't even look like nails anymore.

Like I said, I liked the good old days and the familiar things.

THE GREAT MIDLIFE DIVIDE

I HAVE A FRIEND who has been selling me this ludicrous idea that life begins at forty, with the result that for close to a decade now I have been waiting with bated breath for that momentous occasion when my life will take off. Almost two years past the Big F, I am still waiting, and I must confess that the morale is getting a bit droopy and patience is wearing thin.

In the forties of my dreams I would have a rocking life. Make no mistake: I don't mean vacations in the south of France or romantic holidays on sun-soaked beaches with the Significant Other rubbing suntan lotion on my back and cooing blush-inducing stuff into my willing ears. All I sought were a few romantic drives with the spouse, singing our favourite old Hindi songs, and laughing together. I wanted no champagne, caviar, or cuts of expensive Wagyu beef in Michelin-star restaurants to precede splendid seduction. I would be happy with interesting conversation, a cutting chai and vada pav. I wanted no sparkling solitaire or shopping trips to Milan; I would be just as happy to sit in a park with the spouse and watch the world go by.

Turns out these things are beyond the realm of the adult male imagination. Or, at least, the adult male in my life. I don't know if I am the only woman who goes through this – I suspect not – but the sum total of what the Significant Other wants to do is come home to roost every evening and loll in comfortably tattered 'home clothes'.

Maybe it is that age-old thing of the Cave Man who wanders all day, finding food for the missus and family back home. Maybe men think that their job is done once the salary for the day has been earned. The trouble is, the missus is working too and does not necessarily need support on that front. What she needs is to occasionally put on some make-up, wear a nice dress, and go out dancing or meet up with some interesting folk and engage in some socializing. I suspect it is in their forties that many women realize that the tall, dark, silent guy she was smitten by in her youth has remained just that. Silent. And that silence bites her in the backside every time she resigns herself to one more evening at home watching the telly.

The irony is that the Great Wall of Silence descends on our lives just when we are ready and willing to go out and have some fun because the kids have grown up and flown the nest and we have achieved much in our chosen careers. Now for some fun, we say, smacking our lips in anticipation, but – lo and behold – here comes Grumpy Papa Bear, aka loving spouse, who thinks sipping tea on the balcony is the most romantic thing o the world. It is a lovely thought but, no, it is not romantic or exciting all the time. Thank you. Neither is television foreplay. Thanks again.

I know any number of friends who have run into this Great Midlife Divide. Some have grappled with depression, some have had affairs, some have taken to binge-shopping, and yet others have found their own solutions. I have an older, very wise friend who is light years ahead of me in the ways of relationships. She figured out long ago that no matter how happy a marriage or relationship, each of us is eventually responsible for our individual happiness. Don't put the onus of your fulfilment on anybody else, especially not the spouse, she has always cautioned our group of friends. I have not been too receptive to her message because I wanted to believe that the person we marry can be our partner in everything.

The irony here seems to be that at the very point we women want to go out and let our hair down, the spouse is in the throes of a midlife crisis as well and is looking forward to coming home and being nurtured by his woman. He is tired of proving himself, working his butt off, and worrying about his disappearing hair and libido. He does not want to pull in his rapidly expanding girth to fit into smart threads to go out in the evenings and make small conversation with anyone, leave alone men and women who are perfectly synced and indulging in much PDA.

Now that I have accepted that I alone am responsible for my happiness, I have jumped right into the thick of Project Finding Happiness. And, boy, it has been one hell of an adventure. Over the last few months I have started ticking off the things on my bucket list. As a little girl my biggest joy was to go to the movies and watch the beautiful, curvaceous, fair, pink-cheeked heroines being wooed by handsome men, against the backdrop of snow-capped mountains. I was a plain, mousy girl then and thought my life would always be colourless and drab. Just like me. And so, I would imagine that it was me cavorting across meadows, running around the bushes, and finding love in the arms of cinema's most handsome men. I dreamt of being an actor.

Earlier this year I decided to take the first step towards that dream when I signed up for a theatre workshop and trundled over to join a motley group of men and women who shared my dream of acting. It was not easy, make no mistake about it. Shedding your pride and your inhibitions is way harder at fifty-plus than it is at twenty-five, but even before lunch break I had done two or three turns at miming, drawn a couple of catcalls for my acting, and, hold your breath, been offered a minor part in an indie filmmaker's documentary. OK, it was a mom's role, but who cares? By the time you get to be fifty you learn to pare down your ego, your expectations from the world, and are downright grateful for whatever comes your way.

I have also done several other things for the first time ever: signed up for a Cherial mask-making workshop with a master artisan and I can't tell you how much fun I had getting my hands dirty and fashioning a mask from a mixture of sawdust, tamarind paste, and natural colours extracted from the earth itself. The mask that I made now proudly welcomes visitors to my home and is a reminder to never lose the child in me again.

I have also bonded all over again with my bestie – the one who told me life begins at forty – and have been talking about the stuff that consumes us women as we step into our fifties. The kids have grown up, yes, but our parents have also grown old in the meantime and they need us, she tells me. We talk often about the pain of losing parents – she lost both her parents a decade ago and I lost my dad almost three years ago – and the pain, we tell each other, never goes away. It stays as a dull ache in the heart. 'When your parents go away, you have no option but to grow up because you can no longer run to them with your troubles.' My husband lost his mother recently and I watched him bravely soldier on, as if he had accepted the fact. But that was only until one quiet evening at home when, out of the blue, he dissolved into tears and cried as if the tears would never end. I had never before seen a man cry in anguish and realized that day how much pressure it puts on a man because he has always been taught that real men don't cry.

My friend also tells me it is my duty to be around for the Other Half. Even they have 'men's issues', like women have menopause, and even though you are sometimes so bored you want to just jump off a cliff, it is for you to figure out the shared journey that you set out on with a heart full of dreams, she tells me.

We have made a beginning. Over the last few months we have been doing things together, even if it is watching a movie (his idea, because that saves him from making conversation) or catching up with friends over dinner (my idea, so that he has to make conversation). He has agreed we need to pick up an activity that we both enjoy doing together and these days, post dinner, our dining table turns into our exciting new spot for some action – don't get any funny ideas, I am only speaking about a game of Scrabble which we both love, and which keeps us passionately involved. Someday, I'm hoping that in between sniffing out that smart word that will get me the maximum points, we will also reignite the flame that lost its intensity some time ago. We all live in hope, don't we?

A ONE-SIDED VIEW OF THE WORLD

SOMETHING STRANGE HAS HAPPENED in the world of fashion. And I can't turn a blind eye to it anymore. I started noticing it a couple of years ago when I realized I had not seen one half of my daughter's face in a long time. And no, we don't talk to each other standing sideways.

I'm talking about the new – OK, not-so-new – trend in hairstyles where both boys and girls think that they are only fashion forward if half their face is hidden by hair falling all over it. I think it is called a fringe, though I am not sure of the exact name of this strange trend. What I am sure about is that I don't see the point of this fashion statement that has left half the world's youngsters viewing the world with only one eye.

Don't believe me? Go on Facebook and stalk the young people you know, and you will find that I am speaking the truth. Our youngsters have only a one-sided view of the world. Literally.

My daughter and I don't see eye to eye on her decision to go one-eyed. 'Mom, don't be a drama queen. This is how half the world styles their hair. You just belong to the Dark Ages,' she laughs every time I try to tuck her hair behind her ear. I know she is twenty-six and not a child any longer, but I can't help being a mom.

There are many things wrong about the hair-on-your-face thing young people are heavily into. To begin with I am worried their eyesight will suffer from this fashion trend. When we were kids Achan had a few rules around the house that were not negotiable. No loose hair lying around the face. I had lovely, long, curly hair and they had to be in plaits all the time because he said my eyesight would suffer if I had hair falling on my face constantly. Also, we were not allowed to read in bed because he said that too would strain the eyes. Bad posture would also eventually cause problems with vision and, so, if he caught us slouching on the sofa with our hair loose and reading a book, we were whacked so that we went back to sitting up straight, tucking our hair behind our ears, and reading.

My own worry about the hair-in-the-eye phenomenon is different and it involves Darwin's Theory of Evolution. I must confess, right away, that not having paid attention in science class when this topic was being taught, I can't claim to know too much about it, but I think it has something to do with the modern-day use-it-or-lose-it syndrome. I recall some talk about how organisms change over time because of changes in heritable physical or behavioural traits. Bull's eye!

Now, if this were to be true my fear is that a few generations from now, humankind would be born as a one-eyed species, considering the other eye never got used. And we will, like the apes of yore, grow hair on the unused side of the face.

My good-natured spouse thought me completely loony when I told him about my theory. 'Go read a good book and you will be back to normal soon,' he said, head buried in the newspaper. Someday, when my writing gets me enough money I plan to send him to rehab for addiction to newspapers but given what I make from my profession, it won't be for a long time.

In the meantime, my theory of evolution has evolved in the last couple of months when I have had time to mull over it.

Will the humans of the future also come pre-packaged with earphones plugged into their ears? Considering how few humans I see around me without earphones stuck into their ears these days, it is enough reason for the use-or-lose theory to kick in, isn't it? From what I see, nobody is listening to anybody and everybody is forever listening to whoever is pouring music into their ears, via the earphone. I know adults who go to bed with earphones firmly in place and if that is how much we are dependent on them, maybe nature will just figure out it is easier to grow an earphone in place of the ear that now occupies the side of the human face.

In the same vein, since we now hardly use our fingers other than for typing frantically on keyboards, will our thumb grow horizontally and come padded to protect itself from constantly tapping on the keypad? Will we stop having little fingers because we have no use of them?

And, considering that I read the other day that we are possibly witnessing an epidemic of sexlessness amongst couples, will we be born without our you-know-whats? Just saying.

THE SPECTACLE CONUNDRUM

WHOEVER SAID 'WHAT THE eyes don't see, the heart does not grieve over' has probably never washed her hair with conditioner instead of shampoo, mistaking one for the other. And I can bet my last rupee she has not stood by the wayside like a beached whale, unable to cross the road because she simply cannot see without her glasses.

As you have probably guessed by now, this tome is about my misadventures with my eyesight that has suddenly become temperamental.

When I was twenty and looking out at the world through the proverbial pink-tinted glasses, I had promised myself that I would never become the woman on the local train who wore her reading glasses on a chain across her neck. She would peer out from the top of her glasses and try to strike a conversation with me, little knowing that her grouchy, school principal looks made me feel like a school student all over again, and I did my best to avoid eye contact with her. If I were to meet her today I would apologize because I am in the same boat now and know exactly how it feels.

I would be a glamorous woman at any age, I had promised myself. That was thirty years ago. These days I find myself eating much humble pie when it comes to the matter of reading glasses dangling around the neck. It crept upon me in small bits and bouts, the gradual blurring around the edges of all familiar things. I thought my computer screen had grime on it and so I took to cleaning it in the morning with an LCD screen cleaner. Then I thought my blurred vision was owing to insomnia, which sees me staying up half the night like an owl on sentry duty, but that bubble too burst soon enough when the whimsical old Parsi optician arched his thick eyebrows and said, 'You must be around fifty, madam?'

I winced at the casual cruelty of the grouch, who, obviously, had not noticed that I was trying to be uber cool to impress the dishy guy at the next counter admiring himself in his cool pair of aviators. 'Yes,' I whispered, hoping Dishy Guy had not heard me.

'*Barobarche*. What do you expect at fifty? Time for you to wear glasses, madam. You can see better with them,' Parsi eye doctor said triumphantly.

'He is right, aunty. My mom is probably as old as you and she swears she can see better with glasses,' Dishy Guy said to me from behind his newly acquired aviators. I smiled weakly and scooted off, clenching my fists so I would not punch them both on their smug faces. Did their mothers never tell them that it is the worst etiquette to address unsuspecting women you meet some place as 'aunty'? But that was months ago, and much has happened since then to give me a rather jaundiced view of the world.

To begin with, after much raging and fighting, I have become the woman with the ubiquitous chain that anchors the elusive pair of glasses to the bosom. They hang around my neck most of the time – if I have not left them somewhere safe and forgotten – and they go tappity-tap against my breasts when I rush about hither and thither, doing a million chores. And just when I need them the most, usually when I am at the grocery or medical store trying to read the ingredients on my low-fat, low-sugar purchases or the expiry date on some medicine, I realize they have vamoosed from their perch on my bosom.

That is when I do my panicked-hen routine, as my daughter terms it. Modesty prevents me from groping inside my shirt for the truant glasses, but I sometimes duck behind a store shelf and subject myself to a DIY pat-down to make sure the glasses have not escaped the shackles of the beaded chain and slithered down to get stuck between my mammaries. And if they are not there, I start the Big Dig into the cavernous insides of my It bag.

The thing about It bags is that while most women covet them and carry them like prized possessions, not one of us will admit that they drive us to tears and loss of sanity multiple times a day. My blue It bag is a braided beauty in leather but unlike the popular adage, 'True beauty lies within you', my bag is a nasty creature, a seductress with a dark heart that swallows up everything I own, including my pill box, my stand-by reading glasses, my cellphone, the toothbrush, and the bar of chocolate that I stash away for a dose of guilty pleasure. I even secretly carry a pair of stand-by panties in my bag but that is a story I will come to later.

I have stopped counting the number of times I have scrambled and scrounged around inside the Big Black Hole to find all sorts of missing things, to no avail. Just the other day I went to the salon to do my hair and, as I was getting ready to float out of the place with my trendy blow-dry, I discovered I had neither my glasses nor my purse with me. I looked around in the bag and came up with nothing other than the half-eaten veggie wrap that I had hastily snuck into my bag at the security check while travelling a couple of days ago. Thankfully, my salon has kind-hearted staff and one of them lent me five hundred rupees to pay for my coffee at the meeting I was headed to. The elusive wallet, meanwhile, turned up inside the bag when I was digging around for my missing phone to call my friend to tell her about my predicament on the way home in the cab.

But I am digressing. Right at this moment my main worry is that I am turning into my mother, especially where my glasses are concerned. At seventy, my mother is a woman of great substance. And some of that substance can be found on her glasses, most of the time. I'm talking about stray bits of mustard and cumin, splotches of turmeric or red chilli-tinted oil from when she seasoned the curry for lunch, and traces of sunscreen and moisturizers that she slathers on her face every morning. The thing with Amma is that she keeps complaining her vision is blurred and, we, her three daughters, go crazy each time, worrying her vision is failing due to her long-standing diabetes. The other day we took her to the doctor and Amma explained in great detail that she could hardly ever see and that she worried that the film on her eye was cataract. The kind doctor listened patiently and when she was done, leant across the table, plucked her specs from her nose, and wiped them clean with a soft cloth in his drawer. 'Clean your specs every morning and after you finish cooking and your vision will be fine,' he chuckled. Needless to say, Amma was not charmed by the charming doctor. In fact, she is downright piqued that he robbed her claim to some mysterious ailment of the eyes.

Amma's adventures with her specs are many, and several of our adult memories include images of our late father hot on the trail of her missing spectacles: he was a Sherlock Holmes fan and imbibed most of the wily detective's penchant for dramatics. 'Here it is,' he shouted from the kitchen one day as he made tea for the rest of the family who were slumped on the sofa after hours of hunting for Amma's missing spectacles. We rushed in and there he stood, sugar jar in one hand and her spectacles in the other. How she managed to keep her glasses in a sugar jar was beyond our imagination. In the years since then said spectacles, as hardy a pair as we have seen, have been found quashed under her mattress, in the vegetable tray inside the refrigerator, and, once, in the pocket of a kurta that had been washed in the washing machine that morning!

Not that I should be the one talking about my mother's 'spec-tacular' adventures considering that I have had my own share. I am beginning to think that floor staff at a couple of the neighbourhood malls hide behind the pillars when I arrive at their establishments so that they can escape my manic behaviour.

There is something about the sight of so many hundreds of apparels, trendy, glamorous and absolutely desirable, that makes me want to touch and feel each of them. And, like so many other desperate fifty-something women, I too desire to try them on. And so, I pick out a handful of them and march into the trial room where I avoid eye contact with the trial-room mirrors so that I don't have to see myself in the buff (it helps that I am bat blind) and quickly pull the dress over my head. The problem arises when some of them get stuck midway between my head and my upper region and refuse to come down over my many assets and I have to pound on the door to catch the attention of the person who comes in to rescue me from within the bandage dress which has almost choked me to death. It is then that I start my search for the specs that are lost in my bag and, not finding them, the helpful person has to stay put and read out the price tags of the one dozen dresses that I have no intention of buying.

If you are the same age as me, you know the trials and tribulations of going into a bookstore and trying to buy yourself some good books to read. My routine goes like this:

Go into store, arrive at bookshelves, pick up the nearest book, and read the back cover.

Look up at the bookshelves and have a dizzy spell because your specs are not really meant for distance-reading.

Remove specs, look up at the books, pick one off the shelf, look at the cover, and see nothing at all because you are not wearing specs.

Hunt for specs in bag, find them, put them on and read.

Keep that book down, look up at the bookshelf, dizzy spell…

You get the drift.

My bookstore visit also involves spending a lot of time furtively and very casually searching for my own books on the shelves. I am clueless about the rationale behind book-stacking. I once saw my book, *Legacy*, in the Health and Wellness section of a bookstore chain. *Gifted*, my book on the inspirational lives of people with disabilities, was in the children's section, right next to where gifts and toys are stocked! My job has been to furtively seek those books out and put them back where they belong, and that is a very challenging task if you are half-blind and have forgotten to bring your glasses along. In some bookstores I feel they have set one of their salespersons to tail me furtively because they suspect I am either a pilferer of books or completely cuckoo.

The happy news, however, is that I am not the only one caught in the spectacle conundrum. If you ask other women my age, you will find there are many such chashma-related stories. Over lunch with my gang of lovelies, all in suitably fashionable threads, we laugh at the follies of our failing vision. On a girls' trip out of town, one of them spent an entire day wearing two sets of contact lenses while her friend spent her day blundering around blindly because she simply could not find her lenses. It was past midnight when they returned to the hotel after boisterous partying and when she removed her lenses for the night, she found she was wearing two in each eye. 'What to do, yaar? I forgot I had already worn my lenses and when I saw this pair sitting by the washbasin, I slipped them on assuming they were mine,' she explained.

As for me, the other day I went traipsing to meet this group, making sure to use my brand-new MAC lipstick, Ruby Woo, so that I felt like Mata Hari instead of shoddy me. I was expecting compliments by the dozen but what I got instead were strange looks from the childhood buddies. 'What is with the staring, girls? Have I grown horns?' I asked.

'Not horns, but if you wait one more day, somebody can swing like Tarzan and Jane from your chin hair,' my bestie said to much vociferous laughter around the table. The only silver lining in this scenario was the comfort of knowing that the Old Man who shares the house with me is four years older, and, so, that much more challenged in the vision department. In addition to the fact that we don't see eye to eye on many things, he is unlikely to have seen my luxuriant chin hair.

In the meantime, don't worry if you don't see me around the next few days. I am going to hit the mall searching for a pair of 3X glasses. My friends assure me that getting myself 3X glasses will give me an all-new life. Especially where chin hair and conditioner bottles are concerned. Besides, the optician's store is where all kinds of good-looking men can be found – and my 3X glasses will make the sighting even better!

WHAT LIES UNDERNEATH

THE OTHER DAY I was travelling by bus to some place and there was a G-string in my face. The young woman standing with her hip leaning on the seat in front had decided red hot was her colour for the day and chose to incorporate the sizzling piece of apparel into the lives of everyone on the bus. I am not sure she did it deliberately. A girl has the right to wear whatever she wants. Everyone has; my point is, does her freedom end where my nose begins or am I doomed to spend the rest of my life looking at What Lies Underneath?

I am sure the wise women meant something else when they said it is what lies beneath that matters. I am beginning to think that some of us have taken this so literally that we have brought out all of what lies beneath and are wearing it on our, err, umm, otherwise sensitive bodily parts. Back when I was in my twenties and thirties there used to be parts of the body you were sensitive about and did not mention or display in public.

Don't believe me? When my elder sister and I were teenagers and sprouting signs of femininity, there were clear instructions from Amma to keep those bodily parts covered and off the public radar. Necklines were high, collared shirts and frocks ruled, and dresses extended well below the knee. We knew we had to cover our bosom with a dupatta or with our hands if we had to bend down to pick something up. Knees stayed off limits, we washed our own underwear and never put them out for the world to admire on clotheslines, nor wear them on top of our clothes!

Fast forward a few decades and it is perfectly OK for everyday clothes to comprise, among other things, bralets pretending to be outer wear and dangerously cut shorts that are, quite literally, cheeky. The cleavage that once remained a tantalizing, accidental glimpse or vision now extends to the belly button and nobody cares a damn. It is just another part of your body, right? Growing up, we were told that cleavages were meant to remain covered. Always.

Maybe I am one of those painfully conservative mother hens but even though my fledgling has long flown the coop, I still retain the right to tell her about things she knows not. For instance, the Menon mavens – me and my two sisters – have developed our own secret code to enforce the what-lies-inside-stays-inside policy. My li'l chick and her teenaged cousin know for sure it is time to sit up straight and pull up the T-shirt neckline when she spots three pairs of eyebrows belonging to the Menon women going up and down frantically. A single twitch of the eyebrow is to sit straight, two quick up and down twitches means pull up the neckline, and rolling eyes thrice equates to pull up your jeans. NOW!

I know I live in a brave new world where young men and women have the right to live their lives as they want but I wish this brave new world had parents who were braver and would dare to tell their offspring when and where to draw the line. For instance, no offspring of mine would dare wear jeans that begin halfway past the butt cheek and hang precariously between there and certain embarrassment. 'What if someone stepped on the bottom of his jeans inadvertently?' I asked my offspring the other day, eyeing a guy at a cafe who stood, legs akimbo, possibly to hold up the jeans that revealed a significant portion of pale butt cheeks, and prevent them – the jeans, not the butt – from collapsing in a pool around his ankles.

'Mom! You belong to the sixteenth century,' the daughter fumed, dragging me away from there. Only, this did not help her much because bang in front of us a couple of young women stood nursing drinks, their bosoms ready to pop out of slivers of fabric that seemed too fragile to shoulder their twin responsibilities. You guessed it. Bandage tops with high-waist skirts skimming the floor. Pointless if you, like me, saw what I saw.

'How does that dress even stay up?' I asked, and the fledgling gave me a withering look and said, 'Boob tape, Mom!' I am considerably in the know about the Inside Story now: invisible tape that goes on the bust and inside the dress to lend the perfect off-shoulder dress look. The bonus? No embarrassing n*****s on show.

'Scotch tape had altogether different uses in our times. They were used to hold inanimate objects or things together,' I said weakly, praying desperately the tape manufacturer had done a great job with his production. I did not want the two young things to be mortified because someone at the factory did not put enough hold on the tape, if you know what I mean.

Much water has flown under the bridge since that last discussion with the daughter about all things inside that are now outside. In the last couple of weeks, I have acquired myself a pert new tooshie in place of my decidedly droopy derrière that has seen fifty-plus summers. The trick? Padded, butt-enhancing panties! It is truly what lies underneath that matters.

NO FREELOADERS, PLEASE

THERE WAS A TIME when flattery and a couple of sweet words could get me to do almost anything. I had 'sucker' written across my forehead and there were any number of clever types taking advantage of me. But that was before I hit fifty. No sooner did I cross the milestone than something changed inside me, preventing me from setting myself up for being taken for a ride. These days I have 'FO' written on my forehead and nobody messes with me anymore.

While there are any number of ways in which people have fooled me, the biggest chunk is the people who approach me to 'empower women'. I love women. I am a sucker for anything that will help my ilk because I think that we women have to stand up for each other since no one else will. Anybody who knows me knows that I am game for anything when it comes to the cause of helping a woman.

The trouble is that a lot of cash-rich corporate houses and crafty event managers know this, too, and they are more than happy to come knocking at my doors for some help. For the cause of women's empowerment. What else?

Come February and every year, just as surely as my glinting greys start showing within ten days of an expensive hair colour, my inbox is chock-full of emails from corporate houses, big and small, who want to celebrate International Women's Day.

> Dear Ms Menon,
>
> We would be privileged to have you come to our campus and deliver a keynote address at our annual Women's Day event. You are a source of great inspiration and it would be our honour to have you over. Do let us know about your availability.

In the run-up to International Women's Day there are sure to be at least a couple of emails in my inbox every morning, full of breathless admiration for my work and the boundless inspiration that I provide. I am delighted, of course, to be a source of inspiration. It has been my effort from the time I turned full-time author to write about inspiring people so that we have enough shining examples of what human beings are capable of achieving.

In the past I have fallen for these emails and have ended up wasting my ever-shrinking resources – money and time – to travel to various locations to deliver these talks, often tiring myself out and bringing myself to the brink of a mini financial crisis. Not anymore. I got my wake-up call from a very dear friend, a feisty woman of the world who has been there and done it all, who told me it was time for me to stop being fooled by the world. 'If you don't name your price and put a value on your expertise, no one else will. You have to learn to discuss money,' she had advised. I mulled this over for a couple of months and decided to implement a no-more-freebies policy when it came to spending my time and efforts.

The trouble begins the moment I write the following to my admirers in all those companies – those who cannot wait to have me talking to their female talent pool.

> Dear Ms/Mr...
>
> I would be delighted to deliver the keynote address at your Women's Day event. It has been my constant effort to bring to women stories that will inspire and motivate them to become the best possible version of themselves. My new book, *Devi, Diva or She Devil*, is, in fact, a veritable survival guide for career women…
>
> Please connect me with the person in your team who is steering this event so that I can discuss my professional fee for the speaking assignment. I look forward to hearing from you.
>
> Best regards.

Only, I don't hear from them after that at all. If there is one thing that I have realized over the last few years as an author and chronicler of women's stories, it is this: while there are a few exceptions, most corporate houses who 'celebrate women' have one thing in common – they are as stingy as Uncle Scrooge, if not worse. Either that, or unknown to us, businesses in India, be they Indian or multinationals, are all broke. How else do you explain the fact that they invite people who can boast a decent list of achievements to their name and expect them to spend almost half a day commuting to and fro, all so that they can inspire their employees for free?

> Dear Ms Menon,
>
> Thank you for your kind email. Unfortunately, we have budget constraints for this event and we are wondering if you will be able to do this event for us free of cost. After all, this is an event in line with your area of work.

One corporate house sent this to me recently. Needless to say, I did not spend my time writing back.

A senior executive from the Indian arm of a multinational company that is a household name in the country, called up recently to invite me to conduct a session for their female talent pool. 'We need to inspire them to be able to do their best and make the best of career and personal life. Since your latest book is about that we would love for you to come over and talk about your experiences,' the lady gushed over the phone. 'Of course, we should do that when you happen to be in Mumbai,' she added, knowing well that I live in Pune.

'No, I am not in Mumbai around that time, but I can be if you are interested in having me come over for a session. Why don't you send me a formal email inviting me so that we can discuss my fee?' I replied.

'Oh! I did not know there would be a fee. Why don't you give me an idea of your fee and also put it on an email? I will come back to you with confirmed dates,' the voice over the phone said.

The lady in question works for a company whose revenues in India runs into billions of dollars. Of course, she did not call the next day, nor did she email.

Then there are the ones who will invite you to distant places for the privilege of addressing their employees; they show their magnanimity by providing flight tickets. So here is the drill they expect of you. Wake up at 3 a.m. to be at the airport for a 5.30 a.m. flight, arrive at destination, head straight to campus, have a working lunch with some cheeky HR newbie who hasn't the faintest idea how to be respectful, head to the auditorium, talk to the audience, have a quick cup of bad tea in the office cafeteria, and back to the airport to catch a late-night flight to arrive home past midnight, tattered and tired. And with nothing to show for your trouble. One such company suggested to me some time ago that the goodwill garnered would be priceless!

I am all for inspiring people but the guy at the grocery shop where I buy my dal–chawal insists on being paid. And no, he won't settle for an inspiring talk instead of *rokda*.

Over the years that I have been writing about the journeys of women, I have noticed how timid women are when it comes to negotiating better terms for themselves and how uncomfortable they are when it comes to saying 'no' and asking for their dues. And while my books urge women to stand up for what is right and to take nothing less than what they deserve, what I did not notice was that I was making the same mistakes myself.

Not anymore. This March, I celebrated Women's Day with much gusto because I also celebrated the shedding of my goody-two-shoes, gullible nature and my learning to say a big 'no' to fat-cat freebie hunters. No free lunches from Ms Menon anymore.

This year I addressed a roomful of young women, many of them engineers working with a multinational engineering company, and my heart soared with joy at seeing how passionate and involved they were. I was myself in an inspired mood because I had, finally, quoted my price, stood my ground firmly, and got it. My new motto in life? If it is free, it is not worth my time. My time comes with a price tag. And I am worth it.

OF LOVE, MARRIAGE, AND OTHER THINGS SWEET

It is a sure sign of having stepped firmly into old age when you begin to tear up at pictures of young newly-weds walking into the sunset hand in hand, the love light ablaze in their eyes. Being much married – twice and still alive to tell the tale – I had thought I was well past all the sentimental stuff attached to marriage. With three solid decades of marriage under my belt – both times included – marriage is now more about feeding the family, remembering to pay the cable TV guys, the pressure of socializing with his and my families and other animals, and going to bed. With the hot-water bag. And, oh, did I forget reminding the old man to wear his socks so that his leg cramps don't keep me awake half the night?

And, then, Virushka happened and the romantic in me, somnolent from years of wading through an ageing marriage, wakes up and wonders at the miracle of love. I don't know what it is about that marriage that opened the flood gates of sentimentality in old me. I thought I had been there and done that but just the sight of their radiant, joyous faces when they garlanded each other made my insides go weak and wobbly like the jelly on my belly.

As two of the country's most eligible young people I'm sure they have experienced their share of thrills from relentless wooing by all sorts of equally eligible, well-heeled folks, and for them to somehow find each other from that sea of wannabe suitors is miraculous in itself. I couldn't get over the sheer joy on their faces as they took the vows to be each other's soulmates for life. For want of a better word, it was almost as if they could not believe their luck that this incredible person had fallen in love with them. Did Virushka want to pinch themselves to make sure it was all happening? I don't know but I did feel a twinge of almost-wistfulness at the slow fading away of my young, full-blooded love.

Sigh! It has been a while since I felt that way and I am sure a lot of you in your fifties will readily agree with me. Somewhere in the frantic pace of life, the raising of our children, the quest for better jobs, cars and homes, so many of us have lost the thing that was most important when we set out: the love of our life. The one person we promised to spend our life with, till death do us part.

It is not as if the love light did not shine in my eyes. It did. Back when I was a stick-thin girl of twenty who fell in love with her collegemate and then again, in my late thirties, when I met my current. There were buckets full of love and I drank deep and hard from them but, like I said, between the bills that came calling and the daily decisions of dal, chawal, roti, sabzi and makaan, the tidal wave of love receded, leaving in its place a mere trickle, much like the water supply in many parts of Maximum City.

My friends tell me it is the Virushka destination wedding that has got me all excited and sentimental. Maybe it was all the wine they drank in the vineyards that made them radiate love and maybe they will wake up to cold reality once they have to pick up the tab for the wedding, they reason. I'm not about to buy that argument. My destination wedding the first time was at the marriage registrar's office with its peeling yellow walls, with groups of touts hawking their services standing by the street side; we signed on the dotted line to the incessant cacophony of traffic on busy Bund Garden Road. I got hitched under the unforgiving gaze of a middle-aged registrar who raised his eyebrows and frowned in disapproval that a twenty-one-year-old girl, who could have been his daughter, was about to pledge her troth to an unemployed twenty-six-year-old. Afterwards, we had lunch at Supriya, the Udupi restaurant in Camp, with a couple of friends who witnessed our union and I can vouch even today that we were on top of the world, buzzing with happiness at the prospect of setting up a nest of our own.

I got married again in my late thirties, this time with a wedding party in attendance, some members looking like they were attending a funeral, largely because I was a divorcee with a school-going daughter, but none of the negativity mattered because we were just happy to be getting married. I still remember the orchids on the guests' tables and being surrounded by the love of the few friends who stood by me as I dove into an uncertain future.

I wish I could have held on to the early years of marriage, the quickening of the senses when the partner was around, the way we could look at each other across the room and connect, the way we could laugh together over the silliest things, hold hands and walk around town without a care in the world. I wish I knew what happens to love as we age and forget the rituals of the early days of courtship, the lazing in bed on Sunday mornings, treating each other to ginger tea, vying to be the one to serve the other breakfast in bed. I have forgotten when that stopped and when it became all about leaping out of bed and rushing around trying to achieve the million things that must be done to simply keep the household going.

I doubt Virushka will have to worry about bills to pay and dropping off the kid to school. Come to think of it, the latter image will make one hell of an Insta post for their fans to drool over. Their first anniversary will likely be at some glamorous destination halfway across the world and they will probably gift each other expensive cars and diamonds. Not that the gift matters in the first flush of love. For our first wedding anniversary the then spouse slipped away from home on some pretext and returned to surprise me with a pista-coloured cake, with 'Asha's Freshies' emblazoned across the cardboard box. I was thrilled to bits with the thoughtfulness even though I hated the colour and the name of the bakery reminded me of some other freshies that said Asha would probably be using during a certain time of the month.

The second time over – I mean the first anniversary with the second spouse – I remember being whisked away for a memorable stay at a stately Victorian mansion in the White Mountains, New Hampshire, where Spouse No. 2 splurged big bucks because he remembered I love all things vintage. It was as romantic as it could get, except that the Victorian room was so small we had to sidle in and out to avoid stepping on each other's toes, and the snores from the occupant of the room next door kept me awake all night. The saving grace was the spectacular breakfast the next day, of plates piled high with freshly made pancakes, strawberries and the purest Vermont maple syrup. That and the company of the man I loved, of course.

Virushka will have other challenges, though. For one, they will feel like two celebrity fishes swimming in one giant fishbowl for the rest of their lives. Their every move will be followed by the paparazzi and there will be endless speculation about her pregnancy or, worse, the state of their marriage. If they are sensible – I guess they are because you can't be their kind of successful without being sensible – they will hold the gift of their love close to their hearts, treat the significant other with respect and kindness, and shower them with endless love. In the age of Insta-everything, only this will keep relationships alive and kicking.

As for me I have decided this is the year I will reclaim the romance in our lives. And it will begin with baby steps such as walking hand in hand, slurping ice lolly or eating cotton candy, and laughing at the pink patches it leaves on our faces. Who said romance has anything to do with age?

While on the subject of romance and love, I confess to being completely perplexed about the art of modern-day romances, break-ups and marriages.

I remember a conversation with my teenage daughter sometime ago when I remarked that I no longer saw her close friend hanging out with her steady date of two years. 'Mom! You don't have to marry every boy you date. They were just hanging out. It did not work out.'

'Oh, OK.' My heart sank a bit because when I was a teenager the rules were different. You nursed a broken heart for the longest time over whichever pimply youth to whom your heart had surrendered itself and listened endlessly to Mukesh, Mohammed Rafi, Lata Mangeshkar, and Suraiya sing soulful songs about the pain in their heart over a romance gone wrong. Hell, at least those folks had real romances.

In the suburban Mumbai town where I grew up, there were no real romances because boys and girls were largely not allowed to talk to each other and, even though the air was thick with lovelorn or hormone-laden looks, nothing really came of them. A few emboldened boys would pass love notes to the best-looking girl in school and she would usually turn her nose up and sneer, or, if a guy was lucky, she would stand with him giggling outside the school gate for a couple of seconds. If they both were very, very smitten, they would walk home together, he accompanied by his group of similarly pimply friends and she with her gang of giggly girls. A couple of romances spawned between some of the groupies and soon these 'couples' would make a courageous move and go out for a stolen bhelpuri or panipuri in the only decent restaurant in town. The grand outing possibly cost all of twenty rupees but, remember, that was the entire month's school fee and such luxury dates were very rare.

The mind boggles when I see the courtship rituals of Generation Z. It begins early – I'm told seventh graders have dates – and often ends quickly, and in between these two points are thousands of WhatsApp messages exchanged halfway into the night, Snapchats, and group outings. Teenage sex is rampant, I'm told by doctor friends who often deal with the fallout of the raging hormones but that is another story and, sometimes, the love-struck couple decide to get hitched. But that too is another story and I will come to it soon enough.

Trouble begins when the couple decide to just flaunt their love to one and all – that is fine, too, because the whole world loves a good lover. The trouble is that they decide to flaunt it in the faces of their hapless parents, many of whom don't have the courage to say boo to their offspring. Take the case of a friend of mine, who, at the age of sixty, finally decided that she is ready to slow down, put her feet up, and enjoy her home, after a career spanning forty years. Only that was also the exact time her son decided he was ready to live in with his girlfriend of two years and, before the poor lady could say OMG, the new girlfriend was firmly ensconced in the son's bedroom and the door remained shut most of the time. Which was also fine, my friend told me over tea one day, her hands trembling from the relived trauma, but what drove her round the bend was the behaviour of the loved-up couple: the son emerged every morning from his room to fetch bed tea (made by my friend, of course) for his lady love and, while he was at it, he placed the order for breakfast. His girl loved her eggs fried and could she make it with low salt, he told the mother. The girlfriend emerged from the bedroom at half-past eight, ready to go to work, forked down the breakfast, and left with a cheerful goodbye, leaving my friend to clear up after her.

Weekends were worse, she ranted; the boy emerged at periodic intervals for food and instructed the domestic help to not disturb them. When they were done eating, the tray would be left outside the door, to be cleared, much like people do in hotel rooms. The twosome emerged after 9 p.m., dressed for a night out in town only to return at dawn.

'It has come to such a pass that I want to fling the eggs in his face and spank her for her impudence. I did not retire to slave for my son and his girlfriend. I want my house back, but I am scared he will walk out if I say boo,' she whimpered.

I must admit I'm getting a bit nervous after hearing these stories of modern-day love, especially since the fledgling, back when she was seven, had once declared that she would have four children when she got married and I would have to take care of them while she travelled the world!

PIPSQUEAK ALERT

HI GORGEOUS.

It is 11 p.m. and I am trying to beat a deadline when the chat box pings and distracts me from a rather challenging paragraph I am struggling to write.

Who can it be?

I should have left it alone and focused on writing, instead of letting the curious cat in me take over and check who was pinging me late in the night.

Unknown person (UP): *Hi, this is @E%E^TT.*

Me: *Hello.*

UP: *Sudha, saw you online and just wanted to say hi and that you are so HOT.*

I am not sure if I am to be outraged or should dissolve into helpless laughter because the gem of a comment has come from a terribly young pipsqueak, a friend of a friend who had earlier sent me a friend request on FB. I accepted it only to avoid offending my friend. Big mistake.

I'm outraged on a couple of counts: one, the audacity of the young man; two, his lack of etiquette. What happened to good old manners? Talk about being cheeky!

UP: *I'm coming to your city next week. Let us meet and chat over coffee.*

I don't even remember the last time I went out for coffee with someone. Coffee gives me migraine and I avoid it like the plague. This ill-mannered guy is also giving me a headache. I should avoid him like the plague. But I confess the thought did cross my mind that maybe I should meet him for coffee just so that I can spank him and teach him some manners.

Me: *I don't know you at all. Why should I have coffee with you? Besides, I'm old enough to be your mother. You don't call your mother HOT, do you?*

UP: *What has age got to do with it? Old wine better than new☺. So, can we meet for coffee?*

Me: *Young man, God save the world from the likes of you. I am blocking you now.*

I don't know about the young twit, but I spent a restless night tossing and turning and wondering what the world was coming to. 'Don't worry about such things. The world is made up of all kinds of people,' the spouse mumbled in the middle of the night when I poked him in the rib and recounted my run-in with The Brat.

I did manage to put the incident behind me, even forgetting for a few months that it happened, but that was before I ran into Randy Rambo (RR), also on FB.

It began innocuously enough.

RR: *Hello, Ma'am. This is @E%$R%^R&. I am a fan of your books.*

Instant brownie points, even though his profile pic has him shirtless, staring into the camera with one of those smouldering look-at-me-I'm-so-cool looks.

But, hey, show me an author who does not love getting some book love. Even if it is from a shirtless person with an inflated ego. He has got my brownie points.

Me: *Thank you. Am glad you like my books.*

RR: *Ma'am, I wanted to tell you something else.*

Me: *Yes?*

RR: *Ma'am, in addition to being a model, I'm also a gigolo.*

Long silence. On my part. How do I manage to get into these situations? Panic bout.

RR: *Ma'am, you look so glamorous and you have a happening life. If you or any of your friends need my services, I'm happy to oblige. I'm just a call away. If you give me a list of your friends, I can send them friend requests and we can take it forward from there.*

Stunned silence. On my part again.

I have heard of women who have kitty parties where they invite male strippers to dance on tables and entertain them, but I've never been judgemental about it. In fact, if this is fun, why should only men get to call in escorts and dancers to entertain them? And if I have heard of groups of middle-aged, pot-bellied men going off on stag trips to Thailand (for what else but the Thai massage), I have also heard of gangs of middle-aged, bored housewives who go off on foreign trips where they engage young and willing studs to accompany them. But I have a confession to make. Even though I have been married twice I have had the most boring life ever. The irony is that I am perceived as a woman of the world, largely because I have snagged two men. In parties where the topic of discussion sometimes gets naughty and there are references to cosy threesomes or sex toys, I am more likely to leave the room quickly or spend the evening examining my toes in embarrassment. I have never watched a pornographic movie and neither have I seen a sex toy. There, I have said it. I am fifty-plus and a complete green horn when it comes to 'adult entertainment'. My idea of adult entertainment is playing a game of scrabble in my PJs, before going to bed.

And so, this guy's rather bold offer stumped me. If you presented to me a gift-wrapped gigolo with bulging biceps and such other assets, I would not know what to do with him. Unless, of course, he offered to dust the bookshelf or organize my cupboard.

Me: *Don't contact me again pls. I'm going to block you now.*

I don't know what it is about social media that leads people to conduct themselves in this manner. Do parents know, for instance, that their offspring are prowling on social media, stalking unsuspecting women, and making these awful propositions? Other thoughts crowd the mind: did one of my friends give him my name so that he could befriend me and make this outrageous proposition? Are there people out there who think I need a gigolo? OMG!!

Come to think of it, there are plenty of these sorts outside of social media, in the real world too. The other day I was at the swimming pool, flailing around like a drowning whale, all because my doctor had said that swimming was good for my arthritic limbs. Turns out swimming is dangerous for the rest of me, though, because as I get out of the pool and grab a cover-up to hide the jelly-belly, wet-behind-the-ear dude sitting by the pool pipes up: 'Great job, Aunty. You look gorgeous in the swimsuit!' And this was from someone I had seen running around in his diapers!

'Thanks, son,' I sputter weakly and run for merciful cover in the shower room. I have since stopped going to the pool during daytime. Now I sidle into the pool after sunset, do my exercises super fast, and slink back home, praying hard that I don't meet one more badly behaved young person.

There is only so much a middle-aged babe can take.

SALON WOES

WHEN THE BATHROOM MIRROR recently reflected a decidedly dowdy woman with hair crying out for a dash of colour, I knew it was time for my outing to the neighbourhood salon. Plus, I could do with the idle conversation that we women strike up with perfect strangers in the salon while waiting to be transformed into gorgeous swans. It was only when I reached the salon that I remembered it was their weekly day off and so I trundled off to a glitzier salon with shelves displaying row upon row of glamorous products that made tempting promises to desperate housewives. I was suitably impressed by the sharply dressed young female staff in bright red lipstick and male staff with hair slickly combed back.

The girl at the reception was busy filing her nails while I explained I wanted my hair coloured, my eyebrows done, and maybe waxing, a pedicure and a massage. After what seemed like an eternity, a pretty young thing led me to one of the plush salon chairs where I leaned back so she could give me perfectly arched, diva-like eyebrows.

'Ma'am, your skin is blotchy and dull. You need a chemical peel to brighten it.' When a girl with scarlet talons and red lipstick is hanging inches over your face, you control the instinct to tell her to mind her own business. 'I haven't had a facial in some time,' I mumble weakly and she jumps in for the kill: 'You should avail our skin lightening and laser package for pigmentation. You get a free underarm laser along with our monsoon beauty package.'

My ego already in tatters, I head off to get my dose of happiness from a bottle of hair colour. It is not to be. 'Ma'am, your hair feels like straw,' says a chit of a girl with orange-and-purple hair and piercings on every visible body part. She is holding up my hair for everybody to goggle at and she is not finished yet. 'You need a hair spa and a hair-smoothening treatment. You have too much frizz.' I don't know about smoothening my hair but she has definitely ruffled my feathers by now. Promising to consider her suggestion, I totter to the mezzanine where half a dozen women like me are being subjected to varying degrees of torture. I cringe from the sounds of hot wax strips pulling out hair and insist on a cabin where I can sob in private. Clearly, that is not to be either. In between deftly pulling out hair from various body parts, Chanda, the puller-of-hair informs me that they have services to remove the wrinkles from my arms so they can look younger. She can also refer me to a doctor who can restore my sagging twin assets to their former glory. 'Lots of ladies from your society have availed this doctor's services.'

Barely have I pulled the salon's disposable gown over my body for a relaxing massage when the masseur pipes up. 'Ma'am, you should come for our guaranteed weight-loss package. We can remove the cellulite on your thighs and give you a smooth abdomen. We charge three thousand rupees per kilogram of weight loss,' says desperately-in-need-of-nourishment Anamika.

My stomach does a merry jiggle to some inner music of its own, but I have never thought of my jelly belly as something that has a value of three thousand rupees per kilogram. If it is that valuable, why the hell should I give it away? 'And if you want to make one of your friends sign up, we can give you the package for two thousand rupees per kilogram,' Anamika says, holding out the ultimate carrot.

Lying like a beached whale on that massage table, I never saw the next missile coming – a 'butt facial' to make that part of the anatomy smooth and beach-ready. I confess I was tempted for a moment by the promise of a perky posterior but the thought of alien hands applying a 'fairness mask' on my dimpled backside was too intimidating.

Someday, I am determined to free myself from the tyranny of salon visits, but until then I am looking for tips on how to avoid run-ins with therapists who think my value lies in the fat around my waistline.

STAR-STRUCK

I HAVE IN MY possession a prized dictaphone that some of my friends and a good portion of the female population of this country would possibly kill to get. Friends have offered me, among other things, their homes, their jewellery, and their undying gratitude to make me part with this prized possession.

This is no ordinary dictaphone. This is The Dictaphone. It once sat on superstar Shah Rukh Khan's lap. If I draw it close and inhale I can almost smell his musky cigarette smoke on it, five years after I had my tryst (OK, that might be an exaggeration) with him. I would have to be completely crazy to give it away to somebody else.

Most of the men in the Menon family are convinced we are a cuckoo lot, each one of us women, because we come packed to the gills with eccentricities, oddities and plain idiosyncrasies. How else do you explain that four generations of women in the family, from Amma's octogenarian spinster aunt, to Amma, me and my younger sibling, and our daughters crush on the same man?

You may or may not believe me, but my grand-aunt once lay inert on her bed for almost three days, eschewing water and food and mumbling random things from her younger days so that Amma summoned the extended family to pay their last respects to the matriarch. Thankfully for us and for her, one of the telly channels decided to play *Dilwale Dulhania Le Jayenge* and, within minutes of my having whispered this in her ear, the family relic was sitting with her nose almost into the telly screen, watching her Raj serenading Simran in cold Switzerland. '*Sundaran cherukkan*,' (good-looking boy) she exclaimed soon to my father, who was not so horrified because his own mother had nurtured a giant fan-girl crush on Raj Kapoor and would endlessly narrate the story of *Sangam* to unsuspecting visitors who came calling on her.

But last year, when I crossed the magical Big F milestone, I decided to drop the pretence and bring out the real me, moles, warts, eccentricities and all. After years of being convinced by a dear friend that life begins at forty for a woman, and the damn prediction not coming true for close to a decade, I finally decided to take matters into my hands and make sure that it happens. I am not sure what caused it – obsessive reading of self-help books or the fact that for a long time now I have been getting hot under the collar about constantly having to pretend to be somebody else. I am a simple girl at heart and I am through with pretending to be part of the intelligentsia, whoever or whatever they are.

I love everything that ordinary girls do, including shopping till my feet are ready to fall off, indulging in a little goss (though never any vicious sessions), watch movies and gawk as my favourite Bollywood film heroes fill up the silver screen with their presence. Six packs and man boobs included. If my 'intellectual' friends were to see me slack-jawed and gaping at Shah Rukh Khan or Salman Khan doing their trademark numbers on screen, I would be promptly struck off their guest lists forever.

You see, even though I love my friends to death, there is a great ocean that divides us when it comes to our taste in men, movies, and entertainment options. While they either binge-watch highbrow shows and newscasts on the telly or go to movies that are dark, sombre, and thought-provoking, I prefer joining the masses as they hoot, whistle, dance in the aisles, and enjoy Salman Khan's latest, going hysterical when his shirt comes off and the enormous muscles go on display. I have lost count of the number of times I have lied to my friends that I am out on an interview or meeting, only to sneak into the nearest theatre for the first show of a Salman-starrer!

And, Salman is not even my most favourite. That would be Shah Rukh Khan and I would give more than an arm and a leg to get up, close and personal with him. Am I embarrassed to be declaring this in public at this stage in life? Hell no! The last time I checked there was nothing in the law that prohibits fifty-year-olds from having a king-sized crush on a star.

Which brings me to the other splendid ladies in my family who have had crushes on inaccessible men. My grandma, a feisty, rotund ball on two feet, would wait anxiously for *Filmfare*'s latest issue to arrive on the stands every month. The otherwise strong, independent type would positively chew her nails from the excitement of getting her hands on her most favourite form of entertainment – filmi gossip. She had one favourite in particular: Rajesh Khanna. When the superstar swept *Bobby* star Dimple Kapadia into a whirlwind romance and married her, the entire family, including our grandfather, a bit of a sahib, talked about nothing else. Since she was too embarrassed to go to the newsstand to get her hands on the latest film magazines, each of her four grandchildren got a four-anna coin as a bribe to get her copies of whichever magazine had the superstar's wedding pictures on the cover.

When Prince Charles arrived in India and made that famous visit to the Gateway of India, dinnertime conversations at the household revolved around Padmini Kolhapure's famous peck on the royal cheeks and its propriety. We took sides: Amma thought it outrageous, grandpa turned up his nose at the declining level of mealtime conversation, and grandma thought the girl was made of strong mettle. Under the spell of our star-struck grandma, we kids silently admired the teenager for her, well, balls.

I too have had my share of star-crushing moments that included, among others, Rajendra Kumar and, later, his son Kumar Gaurav. But that was before Shah Rukh Khan arrived on the scene. My life has not been the same since the floppy-haired young man with melting amber eyes wooed his lady love in *DDLJ*. I was already mom to a three-year-old-when he entered our lives but that was never an impediment to my crush on King Khan as he went from strength to strength.

In fact, a few years ago the daughter and I badgered my then spouse to drive us to Panchgani where a very kind friend checked us into the Ravine Hotel where the team was staying as they shot Ashutosh Gowarikar's *Swades*. Jumping around the room from the anticipation of having breakfast with Shah Rukh – having got ourselves a room right below the floor where he was staying – our dreams of a starry meeting spiralled downwards soon enough. SRK had breakfast by himself in his room and nobody could make their way up because his humongous bodyguards stood menacingly at the head of the stairs, as daughter and I found out to our chagrin when we crept up one late afternoon when we heard he was back from shooting early. I tried blustering my way up and even begging a bit but eventually got tired of having a conversation with the skyscraping bodyguard's pert nipples and crept away, tail tucked firmly between my legs.

The bodyguards, however, did not know what we Menon women were made of. We struck pay dirt early next morning when a friendly waiter tipped us off that Khan was now in the hotel gym, working out. Before he knew what had hit him the poor spouse was dragged out of bed, daughter and I were dressed, and we lurked outside the gym where said security guard, he of the firm-nipples-in-my-face fame, threw toxic glares at us. But this time I was determined to not take 'no' for an answer. Our time came at 7 a.m. when the star, looking like a little boy in his gym clothes, surrounded by the Tall Four, emerged, only to be accosted by me and awestruck daughter who stuck her autograph book under his nose as I commanded the spouse to take as many pictures of the momentous occasion as he could.

A gang of other SRK fans had gathered by then and our man was too busy signing other autograph books but even that could not take away from the magic of that moment when I finally got to meet my Raj. Treasured in an old album there is a picture of me and the daughter gaping unabashedly at the Khan while he signs our autograph book. The fan-girl crush and the blazing adulation in my eyes embarrass me today but I confess to occasionally taking out the album and stealing a glance at what was the highlight of that year.

My SRK story continues. Stung by the disappointment of our eyes not having met that first time I swore to myself on the drive back from Panchgani that I would interview the man before I turned forty. I tried every trick in the book, chased after every opportunity to meet him, but missed my goal by years. Then, in 2013, news came that two-wheeler manufacturer Bajaj Auto's Rajiv Bajaj was hosting his good friend Khan at an event where he would address the media about a new collaboration. It was the perfect opportunity for me to keep my promise to myself. Only, by then I had traded in my journalist's hat for a full-time author's and there was no way I could get into that media conference.

The folks who organized the media jamboree, however, did not know my promise to myself or that I had badgered a film journalist friend to connect me with SRK's then manager. To cut a long story short I made it to the press conference and impressed even myself by arriving at the scene, walking down the aisle as a hundred pairs of astonished eyes watched me, and handing over a copy of my book *Legacy* (which contains letters from eminent men and women to their daughters) to an amused Khan who promised to read it to his daughter. I am not sure Rajiv Bajaj was amused by my gate-crashing his press conference but I left the presser floating on air. I am told my copy of *Legacy* holds a place in King Khan's personal library and I can tell you the thought that he might have read it to his daughter warms the cockles of my ageing heart.

But my SRK story does not end with that afternoon either. At 9 p.m. that evening Khan's manager called to say he was meeting a few members of the media at 10 p.m. I convinced the spouse to drive me to the venue and joined half a dozen starry-eyed journos as they waited for the man to arrive. It was well past midnight when he did but I was certainly not complaining because, for twenty-five minutes after that, he held The Dictaphone in his hands, sometimes placing it on his lap, as he recounted his life from playing Hanuman in street plays to becoming India's most beloved superstar. Nothing, simply nothing, can distract the Khan when he is doing his act – an assistant walked in when the interview was on and tied his shoulder-length hair into a pony but he did not take his eyes off me even for a moment. As for me, a lifelong hater of cigarette smoke, I did not notice for the entire hour that he was belching smoke into my face. In fact, I was most reluctant to wash my hands when I got home exhausted but ecstatic, well past 1 a.m.

Lest you think I am the only star-struck woman in the family, let me tell you about my elder sibling, who lives in London and is a brilliant science lecturer. You would have to search high and low to find someone more no-nonsense than her. She loves teaching and her students love her too. We all love her but when my phone pinged a few years ago I was certainly not expecting to see her grinning into the camera phone, as Prince William and Kate Middleton's wedding cavalcade passed by in the background. The smile on her face was priceless, almost as dazzling as Middleton's but what was more priceless was my sister's message that she had arrived at the venue at daybreak and waited patiently with a zillion others, just to catch a glimpse of the new royal couple. *Cinderella stories happen in modern times too*, she wrote.

Why, if that is true, my Cinderella story might just be waiting to happen because this year is when I will meet, interview, and strike up a friendship with M. S. Dhoni. The poor guy does not know it yet but the meeting will happen and he will be the richer for it because my kid sister has enlisted herself for this mission as well. When Dhoni is playing, no one in the house is allowed to either speak loudly or dream of changing the channel. The men prefer to go out and watch the match someplace else because the air at home is thick with conversation about MSD's hair, his shy smile, his biceps, and his cool ways.

Meanwhile, I am badgering this big-shot friend in cricket journalism to facilitate this meeting. I am unsure it will happen as he thinks I am quite menopausal and also cuckoo.

Oh well, we will see…

THE FINE ART OF HOVERING

I AM A HOVERER and I know most Indian women are, too. In fact, I'm seriously considering setting up the Sisterhood of Travelling Hoverers and making myself its mascot-in-chief.

I started hovering when I was about eighteen and have not stopped since; these days, though, the hovering starts much earlier in life – girls now start very young, at maybe the age of three – and then we continue hovering till we are ready to hang up our boots and go off to some hover-free land up above.

Hovering is a fine art, a science and almost a secret female martial arts form. We women keep this between us, talking about it under our breath or out aloud only when we are sure no member of the male species is around. Hovering involves a great deal of patience, stamina, and truckloads of determination. In fact, it is not for the weak-hearted. Or the weak-kneed. I know many women who have given up in frustration because they are too weak-willed but those who have stuck it out, gritting their teeth and holding their breath, know the joy it can deliver.

Among other things, hoverers attain ballerina-like grace and poise, the calmness and zen state of a tai-chi practitioner and the patience and tolerance of a yogi. And the cherry on the cake? Hoverers become the proud owners of a backside that will be the envy of J-Lo, Beyoncé, and Kim Kardashian. Such is the magnificence of the pert, firm, well-rounded butt that comes from a lifetime of hovering diligently.

Intrigued? You should be! Which other form of exercise regimen promises you a pert backside without having to do torturous squats, hundreds of lunges, and undergo other forms of self-inflicted pain? None at all!

It is simple, really. All you need to do to initiate yourself into the world of hovering is to visit a public toilet block the next time you are out of your own home. Enroute to Mumbai on the dazzlingly modern expressway? No problem. On the way to catch a flight for an important business meeting? No worries. The thing about hovering is that you can do it anywhere, anytime, without an expensive gym membership or a personal trainer.

I am not sure where I hover more, at public loos on the road or at airports around the country. I have had hovering sessions at the strangest hours – how is 4 a.m. for a great hovering session? I take really early morning flights sometimes when I am on my book tours or speaking assignments, and while the airports are buzzing with people high on caffeine even at that hour I dare not indulge myself in a hot cuppa. On the wrong side of fifty, I have lost the courage to have coffee or anything liquid when I am travelling because the good old bladder is giving up on me. In fact, I soundly diss all the folks on flights who start making endless trips to the loo just as soon as they board. I know it is none of my business but when your trip to the loo involves poking me in the rib to wake me up so I can make way for you to tinkle – multiple times – it becomes my business. Plus, I have almost had my toes broken from being stepped on by sundry loo-goers, who seem to have made it their business to inflict injury every time they travel.

Now, those of you women who travel economy class and don't have access to fancy airport lounges, know what happens when you head to the ladies' loo. You start mentally prepping yourself five minutes in advance with several deep breaths, you tuck in your tummy, set your jaws in determination, clench your teeth, and push the door open. Sometimes the stench hits you in the face and you flee in horror. Or, if the call of nature won't be denied any longer, you slap a hanky or tissue to your nose and totter to the nearest available cubicle.

This is the moment Mission Hovering starts. You walk in, gingerly look for a hook on the door to hang your bags, once again clench your jaws, and face the truth: there is no way in hell you are going to sit on that filthy pot! The basics of hovering are fairly simple, if you don't let it daunt you. You hitch up the dress, pull down the undergarment covering your modesty, and then position yourself over the pot with the precision of a missile. At no point during this exercise does any part of the posterior come in contact with the surface of the pot. In fact, think once again of those air-to-surface missile attacks. To draw a less intimidating analogy, it would be the loo version of a glute stretch with your entire upper body parallel to the floor, making eye contact with the pools of pee that clueless users of the pot have left behind as their legacy. Positioned like this in airports across the country, I have had the chance to observe hundreds of types of women's feet and their footwear from the bottom of the toilet cubicle. In fact, footwear companies could consult with me to find out what kind of shoes/sandals women on-the-go prefer these days. Also, airport contractors could pick my brain to find out what women who travel want when they are hovering in airport loos. Think lots of tissue paper, hand sanitizers, hooks to hang bags and unwieldy dupattas, and loads of disposable toilet seats. And if humanly possible at all, maintenance staff who are not sleeping on duty inside the toilet blocks.

Coming back to the subject under discussion, though, I suspect that there will soon emerge training schools for hovering. Once upon a time mothers and grandmothers taught their girls skills such as cooking, embroidery, crochet, gardening, flower arrangement, and laying out a good high tea. My mother did not. She did not believe her daughters, or she, needed to know any of these skills other than cooking. But modern-day mothers, poor things, are overworked and have their hands full. I do know a few mothers of young daughters who have taught their girls the art of hovering. A couple of times I have been an unwitting audience to a live demo, as I myself hovered in an airport loo: 'Darling, no! You are not supposed to sit on the pot. You have to spread your legs wide on both sides of the pot and pretend to do a squat like mama does at home. See, like this. And don't wet your panty when you do it. And the pee should be aimed inside the pot. Not outside…' You get the...ahem…flow.

With mothers now too busy with the hundred things they do in their day, I suspect one of those 'How to be a perfect woman/bride' training enterprises will soon include the 'Fine art of hovering' in their curriculum. And so, in between sessions on 'How to host the best cocktail party in town', 'How to have the husband eating out of your hand', and 'How to get your mother-in-law on your side', these entrepreneurs will hold 'How to be the most effective hoverer' sessions. And they will win brownie points aplenty from the students and their mothers for having taught them a precious life skill.

Now that is a good idea for me too. Considering I am a hovering pro like none else – I know all the tricks and moves there are – and considering how little my publishers pay me for writing my books, I should seriously consider setting up one of these training schools myself! And maybe name it Clear Flow Techniques and Strategies Inc.

P.S. Meanwhile, having been told by a friend about a new peeing device that allows women on the move to stand up and pee in the privacy of the loo, I did a quick search and found the GoGirl Female Urination Device on Amazon. It comes with the following instructions: Just hold GoGirl firmly against your body, forming a seal. Aim well and pee!

The device, it says on Amazon, comes with a splash guard. Now, if only the male of the species came with their own splash guard, there would be less mess at home and lesser gnashing of teeth from the spouse. There would be no need then for posters that go 'Gentlemen, don't sprinkle when you tinkle.'

But I don't see myself ordering the GoGirl – available in many colours – anytime soon, largely because I am put off by carrying a device that carries my pee in my purse. Plus, I am not good at online shopping and depend on the spouse for it. When I mentioned the GoGirl device to him he put down the newspaper and laughed like a demented hyena for five minutes straight. Now, I don't have the guts to tell him I might consider buying one.

HOW HAIR COLOUR TAUGHT ME DISCIPLINE

I USED TO BE the most indisciplined person I knew till I discovered hair colour. I have a lot to thank L'Oreal for. Sure, they made me and millions of other women across the world believe that 'we are worth it' but I am sure they never imagined that their product would one day also be given credit for inculcating discipline and keen organizational skills amongst laggards and couch potatoes.

I was in my mid-forties when I first went to the salon to colour my hair and I can tell you it was not an easy decision considering I grew up in a family where a trio of spinster grand-aunts watched over us like hawks. The matriarchs insisted the best thing for hair is to generously slather it with coconut oil every morning and wash it with a gooey juice that emerges after you manically crush hibiscus leaves with your palms. 'When your great-grandma died, she did not have a single white hair because of this magic formula,' they said one time they caught me stealthily carrying a bottle of shampoo into the bathroom of our ancestral home in Kerala.

Well yes, sure, the maternal ancestor did not have white hair. But she also did not have to compete with a gorgeous elder sister for the affection of half a dozen pimply youth in the neighbourhood who followed her around like baa lambs while yours truly sulked in a corner, neglected and forgotten. I thought shampooing my hair would get at least one of the no gooders to fall in love with me but the shampoos of those days, unlike the hair colour brands of today, had no other miraculous properties. They were supposed to shampoo, and they simply did that and left matters of the heart to whoever was supposed to take care of that department. And those people were definitely not doing their work because romance remained non-existent for the better part of my teenage years. And if it did exist, it was only in my head. I fell in love with a lot of good-looking young men, including Kumar Gaurav, but he married someone else and that put paid to any romance in my life.

When I grew up enough to ignore the warnings of the matriarchs, I took to wantonly shampooing my hair, thus inviting prophecies of doom from the trio who said that I would go grey overnight because of the evil chemicals in the shampoo. I spotted my first grey in my mid-thirties, and like so many thousand women do in this country I took to covering them up with henna. Only, I overdid it and by the time I was in my mid-forties I resembled one of those fierce cockerels with flaming red plumage from the cockfighting events that were the highlight of my growing-up years in suburban Bombay of the early 1970s. Nobody likes to wake up in the morning and see a cockerel in bed with them; when I began to suspect that the pained look on Hassled Harry's face had more to do with my rooster impression and less with his andropause, I decided the time had come for me to take the big leap into the world of hair colour.

The first time you see yourself in the salon mirror after your colour job is like the first time you fall in love: you feel the same surge of pure, intense joy in your veins that makes you want to sing and shout from rooftops and tell the world to come admire the object of your love. Only, with hair colour you fall in love with yourself. I sure did. I gasped when I looked at the all-new me, twenty years younger, and had to pinch myself to make sure it was all real. I came home with a song on my lips and even though Hassled Harry had no clue why I was whistling while I heated up dinner – he won't notice it if a nude bombshell made eyes at him – I can assure you there was much energy in the love life that evening. And this from a man who often tells me that we women spend far too much time worrying about hair colour and scooting off to the salon to look lovely. 'Why don't you just let your hair go white gracefully?'

Which brings me to the point under discussion here: how my hair colour made me a disciplined person and gave me other management skills. If you are in your fifties and you colour your hair, there are two parts to your life: one Before Hair Colour (BHC) and the one After Hair Colour (AHC).

Let me begin with the second part first. By the time I hit fifty, I had gathered some smart insights into the hair-colour business. Mine. Not L'Oreal's. I colour my hair the day I have some really important event to attend, such as a speaking assignment, a book launch, or a book reading when I need to be really confident and feeling on top of the world. Right now, my entire feel-good is rooted in my root touch-up. Give me a great root touch-up and I can fight many battles, take on the toughest foe, and deliver talks to an audience of a thousand people. Like Samson, my strength is hidden in my hair. Err, hair colour.

You might think getting my hair coloured is an easy job but hold that thought. It is an event that calls for great planning and management skills. I would make a flowchart and a PPT presentation about it if I knew how to; trust me, it is something that requires planning right down to the last minute. I spend the better part of a week planning the exact date and time I will colour so that I can optimize the two thousand rupees per turn that I pay to transform myself from white to dark brown.

Which is why I am busy as a bee ten days before my hair colour is scheduled – emailing people, requesting appointments to meet the following week, calling up friends to fix lunch dates, and harassing the unsuspecting spouse to make plans for a dinner date or a theatre outing. If you are a girl in your fifties, you will know that it is crucial to pack in as much social life as possible in the first ten to twelve days post hair colour so that you are putting your best face forward on these occasions.

I have my own little priority chart for my AHC phase: the first ten to twelve days post colouring is reserved exclusively for my business meetings, speaking assignments, and hanging out with my glam set. The next week – when my whites are beginning to peek out around the sides of my temple and on my widow's peak – is reserved for childhood friends and not-so-important networking meets. Days nineteen to twenty-five are reserved for ailing relatives/acquaintances in hospital because they are so busy being miserable themselves that they hardly notice the nastily glinting white that has now overtaken the pathetic few strands of black on my head. Days twenty-five to thirty-one I merely sulk at home, avoiding human contact, even advancing my morning walk from 7 a.m. to 6 a.m. when nobody is likely to be startled by the appearance of a decidedly desperate white-haired apparition in our gated community. The last week is also when I am at my nastiest best because I can't bear the sight of the stranger who peers at me in the mirror. By now Hassled Harry has begun to recognize the phase and either stays out for dinner meetings or makes sure there are enough romantic comedies we can watch on telly so that I don't obsess about him noticing my descent from Hot Goddess to Wicked Witch perched on the sofa.

My adventures with hair colour have rendered me Fashion Forward too – last year I got myself gorgeous burgundy highlights thinking I would look like Deepika Padukone, and, while it fell short (literally), I did feel like the glamorous being that I sometimes want to be. I may be wrong, but I suspect that by the time most women are in their forties there is a silent desperation, a deep longing to hold on, even if it were for a little while, to the unlined, unblemished radiance of their younger days. No wonder then that the Indian hair-colour industry is worth an estimated three thousand crore rupees and growing at a healthy pace. You might consider us over the hill if we are fifty and above but what I want to remind the retailers who spend their millions trying to woo the young and the restless is that we are the ones with money in our wallets to splurge.

Hair colour has also given me all sorts of social graces. I am one of those pathetic people who cannot handle a compliment and so, when a kind person would tell me I'm looking gorgeous or that I don't look old enough to be mom to a twenty-six-year-old, I would smile awkwardly and disappear from the scene. These days when somebody compliments me about my looks or comments on my youthful appearance, I tell them the truth. 'Good hair colour,' I declare and they all look at me disbelievingly and say, 'Ma'am, you're very funny.' The ice is thus broken, I spend a pleasant evening and go home floating. I told you, hair colour has done much for me.

In fact, I am so happy with the happiness that my genie in a bottle has given me that I often tell my husband that in lieu of the fact that I never whacked him for a solitaire, expensive foreign holidays, or designer clothes, he has to just do two things for me:

1. Cough up the moolah for a hair transplant job when my receding hairline gets the better of me. If Salman Khan and Shane Warne can do it and get a second life, why should I be left behind?

2. When I finally leave this world and he gets down to organizing my journey into the other world, he will remember to send me off in a blaze of glory, my hair coloured and blow-dried. I have even written down my shades for him – shade 5 with a bit of 5.15 thrown in to intensify the brown. I am very particular when it comes to my hair colour.

THE THING ABOUT THONGS

I DON'T KNOW WHEN the thong became a thing to have in one's possession or when the thong became a thing at all. In fact, having grown up in suburban Mumbai until I was about sixteen I had no clue about a lot of things. Or thongs, for that matter.

My first brush with anything...err...any thong was when I was almost forty and came into contact with a pretty young thing possessing a gorgeous backside. And then some. She lived in Mumbai and had lived in other parts of the world by the time she was in her mid-twenties, and knew everything about, well, everything. The birds and the bees, what to eat, how to eat and look gorgeous at all times...

I was then a fat, frumpy, overworked mother and journalist, and would be dazzled by all that gorgeousness. How did she manage the forever-flushed rosy cheeks; how could she possibly have eyes like a temptress first thing in the morning? I was so busy trying to make breakfast for the school-going daughter that most mornings I looked more like a witch in a tizzy than a temptress. But more than anything else I wondered how she managed to carry off tight white trousers and a minuscule crop top without showing the slightest hint of panty line.

I had and continue to have a thing for white trousers. During my particularly gawky, fresh-off-the-boat days in college I used to be entranced at the sight of this beauteous goddess who would float into class, endless legs encased in white cigarette pants. I wanted to look like her and on my seventeenth birthday I badgered my poor mother into getting me a pair of white trousers. I got an olive-green shirt made to go with it. I thought I would be Goddess No. 2 in class but things went a little differently.

The guy who made the shirt lived in the same suburban town as me and believed girls had no business wearing pants. So, he made my white cigarette pants loose so that it flapped around my ankles making me look like a duck in distress. He also made sure my waist-length shirt was equally loose, but I was no fashionista and knew little about anything back then. When I donned my new outfit and headed out the door, imagining myself to be a drop-dead gorgeous being, my brother rubbed his eyes and said, 'What happened to you?' Thinking him to be jealous I turned up my nose and went off to college, mentally preparing myself to handle all the compliments that would come my way.

I had washed my hair with shikakai soap (there were no TRESemmé or Dove or any other fancy shampoos in those days and if there were, we certainly could not afford them) and wore it loose and, sitting in the 5:55 a.m. local train – along with a dozen fisherwomen on their way to get the first catch of the day – I practised tossing my hair while accepting compliments from my friends.

I walked into class fifteen minutes before the psychology lecture and the silence that met me had to be heard to be believed. 'Happy birthday,' my best friend said, hugging me. 'New dress?'

'Yes,' I preened. 'Birthday gift.'

'Great,' the friend said. 'I'm going to the washroom; do you want to come?'

I went along because I wanted to admire myself in the full-length mirror in the ladies' restroom but no sooner did I get there than Cruella-the-mirror showed me up to be a jackass. And that too on my seventeenth birthday and that too after having haughtily told my father the previous day that I was a grown-up and he could not tell me what to wear and what not to wear. Clearly my white pants should have been on my what-not-to-wear list because what I could immediately see under my shirt and the white pants were my fire-engine red panties. With yellow dots on them. The world, including half a dozen fisherwomen and my principal, whom I had cheerfully wished a good morning (I had wondered why he had hastily looked away as if he had seen a ghost), had seen me showing off my polka-dotted panties. In those days Amma bought our panties and she bought them by the dozen because they were cheaper that way.

'You should go home and change,' my friend said, handing me her long windcheater. I went home and cried and put away the white trousers in a dark corner of our common cupboard. Amma once suggested I could use it as a petticoat under a saree, if I ever wore one, but I was not amused.

Fast forward twenty-three years and here was this Gorgeous Being with whom I was friendly enough to ask whatever I pleased.

'Um…err…how come your panties don't show under your trousers?' I asked tentatively. 'I have to always wear ugly tunics because my panties show through my pants,' I confessed, as she gazed upon me, amusement writ large in the kohl-lined peepers.

'The secret is the thong, darling,' she drawled. 'Have you never worn one?'

'No. Never. What is it?' I asked weakly, already feeling foolish that I had confessed to what was seemingly a huge gap in my knowledge.

'Wait, let me show you one.'

Gorgeous Being returned to show me what seemed like a tiny wisp of clothing to cover a rather large part of the anatomy. But wait a minute, she had forgotten to bring the backside of the panty along. What she was holding up was a wispy, silk thingy – or thongy – no bigger than a handkerchief to cover the front. The back was just a tiny strip of fabric running vertically along the centre of the butt cheeks (Why would anyone call the backside 'cheeks'?).

'Where's the rest of the panties?' I asked, my curiosity piqued.

'This is it, darling. You wear this and the back strap goes inside your booty crack and you slip on your tight trousers and, hey look, no panty lines,' she laughed throatily. 'Get yourself a few. They are life savers.'

I did go to M&S to buy some but realized on the first day of my adventure that this was not my thing...err... thong, for the following reasons.

Thongs are things only for the bold. The entire day that I wore mine – under my nice linen pants – I feared that bereft of the secure confines of my grandma panties, my rather generous backside would collapse and embarrass me in public.

I feared that the world could see the many dimples and the jelly dance of said assets.

I could feel the strap between the cheeks sawing off my insides. Also, what if the strap broke? Would the thong fall down?

As a result, I made sure my backside faced the wall the entire day and later I sidled out of doors so that nobody would see the jelly or the dimples. When I finally got home I wrapped the thong in a newspaper and discreetly disposed of it, praying the guy who collected the trash would not unwrap and check, as he was wont to do. The rest of the pack of five was packed off and put in the attic. Earlier this year I chanced upon them and asked my twenty-six-year-old if she wanted them.

'Mom, those thongs are for grandmas. Throw them away. Who wears skin-coloured thongs anyway?' she chuckled. 'I buy mine only from Victoria's Secret.'

I now know other things about thongs. That they are every girl's coveted possession. That they cost a bomb – the tinier they are, the more expensive they get.

They are to be flaunted; the backside band and waistband come encrusted with crystals and other bling and are meant to be shown off by wearing the thong under low-lying denims.

Thongs attract celebrities and is official outerwear for them. I can think of a few curvaceous divas who have worn it with fishnet stockings and brought the house down at concerts.

Men wear thongs, too, I am told. The purveyor of this nugget of valuable information also named a few worthies who live in various corners of the earth, who have flaunted their thongs and landed many worthy ladies. Apparently, men who wear thongs are guaranteed a great sex life because women get turned on by the sight of hunks in thongs. I had a vision of Hassled Harry in Swarovski-encrusted thongs and had a good laugh.

My only familiarity with men's choice of underwear is from one of the guys in my yoga class whose place was in the row ahead of mine. Every morning, as we practised our *ardhachandrasan*, *trikonasan*, or *veerabhadrasan*, in our effort to connect with our inner being, I encountered this aspiring yogi's inner wear. While said yogi lifted his arms in the warrior pose or stretched himself during *trikonasan*, he was blissfully unaware of the flashing glimpses of his branded underwear, painfully reminding me of my mommy panties, in practical shades of white, grey, beige, and nude.

I hit fifty some time ago and have been ruminating about the lack of adventure in my life. The other day I ran into a sexy, sassy woman of my age flaunting a body-con dress and I could see that she was wearing a thong inside and ever since this thing has been bothering me: dare I go the thong way?

A WARDROBE OF MEMORIES

THE LAST TIME THE fledgling visited was also when I decided it was time to get myself a wardrobe makeover. The spouse had gone off to bed and I was lounging around waiting (actually hyperventilating) for the daughter to come home safely – it was 3 a.m. and there was no sign of the young lady. I was nibbling on a bar of chocolate so that I could prevent the fingers from speed-dialling her while I waited. She arrived at around 3:45 a.m. and almost the first thing she said when I opened the door was, 'Mom! What are you wearing? Is that how you go to bed? It is a wonder you found someone who stays married to you.'

I was stricken, of course. I was wearing my favourite pair of PJs – the one with colourful prints of chocolates and ice-cream cones – which I had bought in a fit of enthusiasm in 2010 and had adopted as my second skin. I admit they were a bit frayed – OK, not frayed, they were tattered in some places – but you don't toss away everything old, do you?

'What is wrong with these pants? They are the most comfortable pair of PJs in the world,' I said to her. 'And don't distract me by changing the subject. You are home very, very late and it is not a safe world out there.'

'Of course they are comfortable, but I must warn you that if you wear them any more you might be poorer by one more spouse or friend-zoned permanently. Also, Mommy, I'm a twenty-six-year-old adult and you don't have to stay up and wait for me to come home!'

I would tell the fledgling when raising her that parents can be your best friends and, therefore, can't blame her if she wants to give me friendly advice.

'Yeah, but I like them,' I murmured, and she replied, 'Mom, throw away all those outfits you have been wearing for the last fifty years. Or, does it only seem like that long? Go get yourself some new clothes. And get yourself a life!'

Having spent the remaining few hours of the night mulling over the wise fledgling's well-meant advice, I attacked the wardrobe first thing in the morning and here is what I found:

Six off-white handloom kurtas cut in the same style: V-neck and three-quarter sleeves.

Six churidars made of the same fabric.

Eighteen beautiful block-printed dupattas lovingly made by my dear friend, Indira Broker. I'm sure she did not mean them to be worn for eighteen years but I can't bear to let them go.

Six pairs of jeans ranging from sizes ten to fourteen, bought over the years to fit my widening figure and worn possibly once every six months. I can no longer bear anything that clings to me. Not jeans. Not spouse. Not any other form of life.

Twelve white tops, six of them with the price tags still on. I'm not sure why they are still in my cupboard because they are all size eight; I probably bought them in one of my optimistic moods when I thought I still had the will power to hit the gym and lose some weight.

Six sets of lingerie, each sexier than the other, in midnight blue, luscious red, shocking pink, sensuous black, etc., bought on my trips abroad when I miss the Significant Other and commit to add some sizzle to the married life when I get back home. The thing is when I do get back home I am so relieved to be in my own bed that I sleep through the next five nights in my faithful old PJs, and by the time the sixth night arrives I have safely put the sexy lingerie away for another time. I suspect, sometimes, that the old man is relieved I live in my old PJs. No pressure to rise to the occasion.

There are also thirty-five saree blouses (these are in addition to the twenty-five I have stowed away under the bed), in khadi, handloom, and silk, and in the most gorgeous shades ever. The trouble, however, is that most of them don't fit, thanks to my tailor from hell with whom I share a love–hate relationship. The young man in question was trained by my original tailor, a wonderful man who passed away a few years ago, leaving as his legacy this young fellow. Our man is the kind of man you only read about in books. He has customers by the dozen who flock to him due to his considerable talent but believes in the slow life: the last time I saw him was about six months ago when he disappeared with half a dozen blouse pieces and some fabric for a couple of summer dresses that I wanted to wear when the weather turned too hot.

The other problem with him is that he is cocky as hell and does not believe in taking measurements. Every time I hand him a few things to stitch, he refuses to take measurements, insisting that he remembers my measurements (!) but when the garments arrive and I try them on, breathless with anticipation, I find they have either been stitched to fit a pregnant rhino or a twiggy. By now I have learnt to just take a deep breath and add the garment to the increasing pile of blouses I cannot wear. I only have three blouses that fit me and those have been stitched not by him but by his dear, departed boss, and that means they have been around a long time now. Why, I wore them the other day and someone remarked how trendy I had become because the high-neck, retro blouse is all the rage now and how come I had become so style-conscious... I chose to not respond but exulted within because, finally, I had something stylish in my wardrobe, even though it was stitched in 1998.

I found other stuff in my wardrobe too. Five crisp old five-hundred-rupee notes that I had spirited away from the monthly budget, now rendered useless, thanks to demonetization. Six pairs of earrings in a box that also contained twenty-five different buttons to be stitched onto God-alone-knows which new dresses. A pair of scissors that had gone missing from the kitchen. One dozen stoles, never worn because I am not cool enough to wear stoles. A stack of receipts of all the clothes that I buy and can never muster the courage to wear. A card on which I had scribbled a love note to the Significant Other but had forgotten to give him. I had read somewhere that smart women keep their men interested by doing all sorts of romantic things such as tucking away a naughty love note into the lunchbox so that he would think of you at lunch and come home in a romantic mood. I bought the card and wrote him a note but realized too late that because I never pack him any lunch I would not be able to tuck it into the lunchbox. I must now find another way to get the note to him. Maybe I will google 'Top 10 ways to slip a sexy note to your significant other'.

Also in the wardrobe, on the lowest shelf where I have folders full of documents that I don't know what to do with, were the following:

An old, faded drawing by my then four-year-old showing two stick-figures: a tall one with long, flowing hair and a tiny one with tinier hands, their stick-fingers intertwined, walking into the sunset. *To the best mama in the world. I love you*, it read.

A dozen old albums bursting with sepia-tinted images and memories from the past. And a precious, more recent one. Amma and Achan on their fiftieth anniversary, he grinning as if relishing a secret joke and she, standing beside him, smiling shyly into the camera, happy to just be in the warmth of the man she married at the age of sixteen. She never knew he would leave her and all of us just two heartbreakingly short years later. For her that moment was eternity.

A picture of a twenty-five-year-old me and my two sisters clucking and cooing at my tiny tot on her first birthday. The fledgling says it is her greatest joy to have these two aunts in her life, but they are also the biggest challenge to any love life she might ever expect to have, considering that any man she might meet will have to pass muster with those two. And Amma. Not to mention me.

A picture of the fledgling with her father, he looking at her in amazement as if he could not believe she was his. And she, all of one, looking into his eyes and smiling a thousand-watt smile that could light up a town. They still look at each other like that and nothing can take away that mutual admiration.

A picture of me the day I married the second time and, suddenly, I relived all the fears that haunted the thirty-eight-year-old me right up to the day I decided to commit myself to another man. Was I being selfish and unthinking in doing this? Would I end up hurting my little girl? Would my parents ever forgive me for putting them through the horror of a divorce and then a remarriage? Would I ever find happiness again?

Sitting there on the floor of my bedroom that morning, the sun filtering in through the wide windows and the chirping of the hundred birds filling the air, I knew one thing for sure: the young woman who was fast asleep in the room across from mine loved me more than I ever deserved, my parents had long forgiven me and embraced Spouse No. 2 as their own son and I had managed to keep my divorce from the first husband graceful and pleasant so that there was no bitter separation but a gentle branching away. All was well with our world and it was largely because, no matter what had happened in our lives, we had stuck to the good old values of honesty, kindness, love, and respect for each other. We need all of that much more than we need sexy lingerie and a new wardrobe. I don't need to get myself a life with new clothes. I already have a life and it is full of the people I love and the memories that I have created. I am amazed at how my life envelopes me in love and warmth. Just like my old PJs.

A TRIP DOWN MEMORY LANE

WE WERE OUT SHOPPING for our weekly groceries – a rare occasion when I decided to set out on this adventure – when I saw Hassled Harry head to the far end of the store where the shelves were full of Diwali staples, including brightly painted diyas, fragrant agarbattis, fancy *kandeel*s, and such other items. He loves grocery shopping because he claims it de-stresses him and so I did not pay heed when he slipped a couple of little somethings into the shopping cart.

It was when we were putting away all the purchases that I noticed him quickly grab a mysterious packet and spirit it away. Upon enquiring he squirmed and sheepishly revealed that he had picked up a packet of *utna* and a Mysore Sandal soap. 'Mom used to give us a bath with it at the crack of dawn every Diwali,' he said. 'Diwali does not feel the same without a fragrant *utne* bath.'

Coming from a fifty-four-year-old this might seem strange to most people, but I get it. Totally. Growing old does not mean that memories cease to exist or that we forget the little rituals and ceremonies that make up the rich tapestry of our lives. My spouse's Diwali memory is of a house awash with the laughter of his large, extended family, sitting around their modest dining table and enjoying Diwali *pharal*, the highlight of which was his mother's signature *gulkandache kanole* – delicate *karanji*s with a stuffing of *khawa* and *gulkand* – which had the family clamouring for more.

I was passing by sweetmeat-maker Chitale's new store on NIBM Road a couple of days before Diwali when my insides crumbled a bit and my breath caught in my chest as if a giant fist was squeezing the life out of me. In a split second the pretence I had been putting up of being a happy woman, content with her lot, gave way to a grey misery that I knew I had to hide because I did not want to spread it around.

All it took to reduce me to a teary mess was the sight of a large tray of gorgeous, golden-yellow *sajuktoopatle motichoor laddoos* sitting on the counter, waiting to be picked up and devoured. My father and I shared a great love for the sinful, calorie-ridden *laddoo* and would often out-eat each other when there was a box around.

I had called my father two Diwalis ago and asked him – as I was used to doing everytime I travelled from Pune to Mumbai – what he wanted from Pune. 'Get me those motichoor laddoos,' he had replied. Achan had a sweet tooth like no one else I know. All his life he ate healthy food, avoided fried and excessively spicy food, ate lots of fruits and nuts, and was a fitness freak; but when it came to sweets he simply had no control. He could polish off a large Toblerone bar in two days, eat Lindt chocolates with as much relish as Amma's sheera or payasam, and would eagerly wait for the desserts to arrive at the table when the family went out for dinner.

His love for the Chitale laddoos was a standing joke in the family. He would open the box with childlike glee and grab a few before stashing the box away at the bottom of the fridge so that Amma would not give his prized possessions to casual visitors. Achan had a peculiar way of eating the laddoos. He would hold three laddoos in his right hand – two of them nestled in the centre of his palm while he finished the first one off, as though he worried we would make off with them if he left them on the table.

My box of laddoos never got eaten that year and stayed in the fridge, forgotten, for a long time. Achan fell ill during Diwali and had to be hospitalized. I reminded him of the laddoos as he lay on his hospital bed, and his eyes lit up. 'I will be home in a couple of days. Don't eat them up.' Achan passed away two months later, slipping away from us as we watched helplessly. The laddoos lay hidden and forgotten. It was the hardest thing to discard when we finally discovered his stash of chocolates and laddoos in the fridge.

Last year I could not bring myself to buy those laddoos. Now that he is gone, strangely enough, so is my fondness for sweet treats.

As for the rituals of Diwali, I have made a mental note to myself: next year Hassled Harry gets his *utne* bath and the *kanoles* made by yours truly. Last year, even though I sorely missed my beloved Achan, I continued with my Diwali rituals with my daughter: wearing a nice saree, lighting up the house with lamps and decorating with fresh flowers just before dusk, performing a small pooja, and spending time together, bonding as a family.

He would have wanted it that way.

FORGETTING AND REMEMBERING

MEMORY IS A TREACHEROUS thing. It steals upon you unbidden when you are going about your daily chores and lands you a sucker punch in the solar plexus.

The other day I was sitting on my usual perch in the balcony, sipping chai and watching the world go by, when I caught sight of a father–daughter duo down by the kids' play area. He picked her up and tossed her into the air and the evening reverberated with her delighted squeals of excitement as he gathered her into his arms and held her close.

The memories of my own childhood came gushing forward, of Sundays spent clambering up the guava tree in our garden to pluck the plump yellow-green fruit and throwing it down to Achan who would stand below, catching each fruit nimbly in his faded lungi, and piling them in a corner of our walled garden.

Sunday mornings were all about being in the garden with him as he pottered amongst his many rose bushes, humming his favourite Mukesh songs, systematically going through each bush to check under the leaves for worms that could destroy an entire bush in a single day. We would hang around waiting for instructions from him; sometimes he allowed us to pluck the roses that were past their prime and to pull the petals off them carefully so that Amma could make heavenly *gulkand* out of them. She would bring out her sparkling glass jars and line the insides with the petals, top them with sugar, and leave them in the garden for the entire week, letting the sun melt the sugar which would be soaked up by the petals until it all came together in a glorious burst of rose-flavoured awesomeness that we had with our milk every morning. I preferred mine as an after-school snack, applied on a warm roti, rolled up, and relished to the last morsel.

Some days I would steal into the kitchen when Amma was not looking and dip my finger into the *gulkand* jar, scooping the golden-pink syrup into my mouth, licking my finger till the last trace of my ill-gotten gain had disappeared.

Life was simpler back then and even though it was Amma who raised us, it was Achan who was our hero, the parent who stood waving to us from the back of the goods train that went past our little cottage by the railway track. He was a guard in the railways and my heart swelled with pride to see him in his white uniform.

'Do you know my father has to give his permission before the driver is able to take the train to the next station?' I would preen in front of the children of other railwaymen who lived in the community and that would set off a minor war with each of them claiming supremacy for their respective fathers. The father of one of the girls was a motorman and I had a running feud with her because she insisted her father was a bigger hero since a train would not move if her father did not drive it. I remember pulling her pigtails once when she insisted her father was one up on mine and her kicking me on the shin and the two of us rolling in the mud, screeching like angry roosters, till the rest of the gang came and separated us.

Sunday was also when Achan treated himself to a hot oil massage so that his muscles gleamed in the morning sun when he pottered about in the garden. The four of us waited around like fond puppies, watching him pick up weights and lift the bulwark. I might have been four and my brother around three, when he picked us up and turned us into human weights, one child on each of his biceps. To this day I can remember the pride I felt to be his daughter when a couple of my friends, who happened to witness the feat, narrated it to the rest of the scraggly gang of girls and boys from the colony.

My cup of tea lay forgotten that evening as the memory of my father transported me to the early days with my own fledgling. To the first time I held her close to me, when she'd spent all of five minutes in this world. When the kind nurse thrust my baby into my arms, I was too tired after a marathon thirty-two-hour labour to want anything to do with anyone else. I simply wanted to be left alone to sleep and I did, almost immediately after I had held the slippery bundle for a minute and noticed her enormous eyes. Maybe my memory is playing games with me, but I remember looking into a pair of the most trusting eyes ever and forging a bond with her that has stayed with us through a lot of ups and downs in our lives, including my separation from her beloved father.

Just before I dozed off on that winter afternoon in the government-hospital bed, I had already named her Nayantara, the one with eyes like stars. It has been over a quarter of a century since she first gripped my little finger like her life depended on it and I know that even now it is me she reaches out to when there is the slightest hint of trouble in her life. Some bonds are made in heaven and a daughter's bond with her mother is the first on that list. Which is not to say that the fledgling does not use her deer eyes to con me occasionally and take the last rupee off me. She does. And I always fall for it. But then that is what moms are for, isn't it?

They say it is the memories that we hold close to us that allow us to stay sane and keep us company in our old age when the rest of the world no longer has time for us. I remember my mom's aunt who lived with us the last few years of her life. She woke up one day and Amma said she had forgotten everything about her present life. All she remembered was her life back when she was in her twenties and had travelled from her ancestral home in Kerala to Mumbai, training to be a nurse, and working with a wonderful, kind-hearted doctor in Mumbai who treated her as part of his family. For over three years my grand-aunt, Meenakshiamma, wandered around our Mumbai apartment, addressing my father as Dr Joshi and talking at length to him about various patients. She addressed us by strange names, spoke about ailments and treatments, and cautioned Amma occasionally about the stranger who came into the house and hugged her youngest daughter. The stranger was my father and it was his ritual to come home and hug my kid sister, the apple of his eye. Sometimes, he would sit with Meenakshiamma and discuss the patient she had tended to that day. She was happy as a lark after that and my father was happier still because he had brought some happiness into the life of a woman he adored.

Memory is also a great friend to have on your side. Amma came visiting me last year, around the same time that I was preparing for one of my Get Writing workshops. As I put my presentation together for a class of aspiring writers, she asked me, 'Can you teach me to write? I am old, but I have a lot of stories that I want to tell.' And there it was, just the thing the doctor ordered for her condition: something to keep her active mind occupied and give her a sense of purpose.

'Of course you can write, Amma. Your stories will shine because of the experiences that you are carrying around in your head. Let us begin tomorrow,' I replied.

Amma stayed with me for fifteen days last year – for the first time in the twenty-eight years since I married and left home – and she was like a child who had discovered a precious new toy or a storybook. She took to writing like fish to water. Gone was the woman who dragged herself from room to room, staring into space, or simply sunk into depression, and in her place was an enthusiastic woman who drove me crazy with a million ideas of what she wanted to write. In the end she managed to convince me that she would write about her experiences of living with Achan, the man who had devoted his entire life to the welfare of lakhs of railways workers in India. I worried that the memories would send her spinning back into depression, but I had not accounted for her nerves of steel, of her refusal to be cowed down by circumstances. Every morning, as soon as my husband left for work, we would settle down at the work desk and she would dig into her bag of memories and come up with a stream of recollections, some of them clear and lucid, some a bit garbled, but each relating to a phase of their life together.

Achan, or CR as he was called by lakhs of workers across India's railway network, was one of the key leaders of the railway strike of 1974. Responsible for leveraging the collective strength of seventeen lakh workers and motivating them to join the strike, he was on the radar of the then Indira Gandhi–led Congress government, which used everything in its power to suppress the movement by hunting the leaders down and throwing them in jail.

In the summer Amma wrote her book, I spent long hours listening with rapt attention as she spoke to me about things I had experienced as an eight-year-old but the significance of which I had never understood. She spoke to me about Achan going underground to avoid arrest so that he could continue to keep the morale of the striking workers high, against the backdrop of the government using brute force to strangle the strike. She spoke of her struggle to feed her four children with no resources and a missing husband. She wept as she spoke of midnight knocks on our door and of policemen barging in to look for Achan; she laughed when she remembered how other policemen, who were sympathetic to the railway workers' cause and admired Achan, would forewarn her of the impending raid so that Achan would stay away from home that night. Tears flowed unfettered when Amma spoke about Achan's arrest and the time she took us to meet him at the infamous Arthur Road Jail, where they threw him into the company of undertrials, many of them seasoned convicts. And then her mood turned dramatically as she spoke of his release, the protracted legal struggle to get justice for the hundreds of rail workers who had been dismissed during the strike, and their eventual triumph when the court categorically ruled in their favour.

It was a season of healing for both Amma and me as we bridged the distance that had surfaced between us since I moved away, after getting married, to another city and got busy with my career and raising my only child. For Amma it was both therapeutic and liberating to talk about her life with Achan.

In the six months that followed our summer of conversations, Amma surprised us all with her commitment to her new-found cause. She was up at daybreak and at her desk, writing page after page about their shared journey. My telephone rang endlessly – at daybreak and at midnight – as she called to check if she could write about specific incidents in their life, sometimes ticking me off for failing to read through her weekly writing in time for her to revise. Months into her new-found passion, Amma called me up in the middle of one afternoon to say her story was complete. On 23 February 2017, Amma stood proudly on the dais and unveiled the first copy of her book, *My Journey with Comrade CR*, to thunderous applause from hundreds of his admirers and railway colleagues gathered to remember Achan on the first anniversary of his passing. The mid-morning air was thick with slogans of '*Comrade CR amar rahe*' and she beamed with happiness.

And now that the giant tap of her memory has been opened, the memories are gushing out fast and furious as she fills up journal after journal, and page after page for her new book about growing up in her ancestral home in Kerala. And our extended family is waiting with bated breath to read it.

THE FAMILY THAT EATS OUT TOGETHER

YOU WOULD THINK GOING out for a meal is a piece of cake. Just walk into a nice restaurant. Order like gluttons, stuff yourself with pizza, pasta, and dessert. Leave. No tedious chopping, grinding, and cleaning up afterwards. Pure bliss.

But not in our household. Going out to eat with my extended family is like third-degree torture. It is a mind-bending experience at the end of which we all go to our respective corners in the house and curl up, our insides quivering, and pray that there is no family meal plan for a long time. I don't know about the rest, but I certainly do the above.

And so would you, if the entire ritual went like this.

Project Eating Out: Phase I

Me: 'Let us have dinner out today.'

Spouse: 'Shit! Why? There will be so much traffic outside. Plus, parking is always a problem.'

Me: 'That can't be your excuse for fifteen years!'

Spouse: 'OK. Whatever.'

Fledgling: 'Mom! You can't just spring a plan on me at the last moment. I have to go out with friends.'

Kid sister: 'But this is the first time in months we are going out as a family. You better cancel with your friends.'

Fledgling: 'OK. But who goes out with family on weekends?'

Me: 'Don't be such a grouch.'

Amma: 'Why go out? There is so much sambar and rice left over from lunch. Outside food is unhealthy and expensive. I can cook some avial and we can all eat at home.'

All of us in unison, thinking of the cleaning-up horror post Amma in the kitchen: 'No. No. No. Let us please eat out.'

Project Eating Out: Phase II

Me: 'What would you like to eat?'

Spouse: 'Anything.'

Fledgling: 'Anything.'

Sister: 'Anything.'

Niece: 'I want to eat pasta.'

Fledgling: 'Let us go to Fancy Restaurant A.'

Me: 'But that is frightfully expensive.'

Fledgling: 'Mom, that is not expensive. That is how much eating out costs.' (Withering look plus eye roll.)

Amma: 'I'm not eating pasta. Why eat tasteless, bland food? I want to eat idli and dosa in Matunga.'

Fledgling: 'Ammamma, you eat idli and dosa every single day at home! Why do you want to have it for dinner too?'

Niece: 'OK. Let us go to Restaurant They-Serve-It-All. She can have idli–dosa and we can have spicy chicken.'

Fledgling: 'So boring. I don't want to eat Indian. Let us go to Fancy Restaurant A.'

Sister: 'Enough now. We are going to Restaurant They-Serve-It-All. Everybody gets to eat what they want. Now get ready quickly and let us go.'

One hour and four changes of outfits (Amma), much hyperventilating (me), much sulking (fledgling and niece), much honking and cursing by the driver of the evening (spouse) later, we arrive at the restaurant to be greeted by a thirty-minute wait to be seated.

Me (eyeing gang of girls and boys blowing smoke rings): 'Smoking is not allowed in public. It gives me a migraine. Can we tell them to move away?'

Fledgling: 'No. We can't. It's a free country. Besides, how does it matter to you if it is harmful to their health?'(Eye roll.)

Me: 'Passive smoking kills too. I am within my rights to tell them to stop smoking in my face.'

Amma: 'This is why your BP is always high. Stop minding other people's business.'

Half an hour and much complaining later we are seated. Next to a table of twelve noisy revellers and four kids who are attempting to kill each other with the cutlery. The youngest of the four is standing on the table and throwing the mother-of-all-tantrums.

Me (to the waiter): 'Can we have another table please? This is so noisy.'

Waiter: 'Sorry, ma'am. The restaurant is full.'

Me: 'But why should we suffer this noise? We have come here to enjoy, and hearing four kids shriek is not entertainment.'

Waiter: 'Ma'am, sorry. What can we do? Other guests have complained too but these guests got angry when I requested them to please mind the children.'

Me: 'I should have sat at home and eaten instead of paying through my nose to suffer this chaos.'

Project Eating Out: Phase III; Or, When the Food Arrives

Amma: 'My sambar tastes strange. Do you think they made it in the same pan they use to make their non-vegetarian food? And what is that brown piece floating on the surface? Is it chicken?'

Me: 'Amma, no, it is not chicken. It is pumpkin. And no, restaurants use separate vessels to cook vegetarian food.'

Amma: 'And I make better dosas than what they have served here for a hundred and eighty rupees. There is a kid behind me who is kicking the back of my chair non-stop. But don't say anything to them. Let it be.'

Waiter starts serving the food. The trouble is every time he stretches his arms to serve someone sitting across the table, his armpit is in my face and the experience is enough to knock me out.

Me (to waiter): 'Can you please go around the table and serve? That will be easier.'

Waiter: 'Ma'am, I can do it like this too. Don't worry, ma'am.'

Me: 'Yes, but can you please go around and serve? Your sleeve is in my dal at this very moment. And you are leaning into my face every time you serve someone on the other side.'

Waiter: 'Sorry, ma'am. I will go around the table next time.' (Exits hastily.)

Fledgling: 'Mom! You did not have to tell him that. He must be so hurt.'

Me: 'Yeah, but I was about to pass out from the smell of his armpits. Also, his shirt sleeve was dirty, and it was in the dal.' (Fledgling rolls her eyes.)

The kids at the next table, meanwhile, are now running around our table chasing each other, until one of them suddenly decides to duck under the table to hide. We are soon trying to eat our meal with four pesky kids hiding under the table and, no doubt, planning their next step.

Ouch! One of them has just poked me on the toe with a pointed object, and I have had enough.

Me (to the parents of the kids who are enjoying their wine): 'Excuse me, could you please get your kids out from under our table? One of them is jabbing me with a fork.'

Scowling mother of kid: 'Oh, are they under your table? Sorry about that but kids will be kids.'

Me: 'Yes, but they are your kids. Please take them away.'

Mother of kids: 'Do you not have any kids? They are often mischievous.' (Rolls eyes and screeches for kids to come out. They do. And promptly start running around the table again.)

Fledgling: 'Mom. Stop it now. They are not your kids. You are not responsible for them, so don't start disciplining them.'

Spouse: 'Kids will be kids.'

Me (to spouse and fledgling): 'Neither of you has the guts to say boo to anyone.'

Fledgling: 'This is not about saying boo. This is about not being rude to people. It is so embarrassing.' (Eye roll.)

Me: 'OK. OK. Sorry. End of topic... This place is so hot. And why is the music so loud?'

Fledgling: 'The music is not loud. This is how you listen to music.'

Spouse: 'And it is not hot. I am almost freezing.'

Me (to waiter): 'It is so hot here. Could you lower the temperature please?'

Waiter: 'Ma'am, we are already at eighteen degrees. Cannot lower any further.'

Me (to waiter): 'Are you sure? I'm sweating.'

Waiter: 'Ma'am, other guests are complaining that it's too cold.' (Scurries away.)

Fledgling: 'Mom, we understand you are menopausal, but the rest of the world does not care. Please don't be a drama queen. This is why I never go anywhere with you. People are frightened of you.' (Eye roll.)

Me: 'OK. OK, so I am menopausal, and you will get there too. I won't be around then but you will remember this conversation.' (Where I dissolve into tears and a puddle of hot flush-induced sweat.)

Needless to say, there is a chill in the air on the ride home after dinner. And it isn't from the car's AC. It is me giving everyone the cold shoulder.

SAYING GOODBYE

WHEN MY SISTER RELEASED her hold and gently set my father's favourite red T-shirt on its onward journey in the roaring blue waters of the Ganga in Rishikesh, her heart broke into a million pieces, she said to me afterwards. When she finally and painfully summoned the courage to let go of our recently deceased father's most favourite possession of all – his red T-shirt – I think she left her childhood behind and became part of the rest of us grown-ups in the family.

When he passed away from a brief illness at the end of February two years ago, our world collapsed around us. At eighty-three, he was one of the fittest men we knew; he had a healthy lifestyle none of us could ever manage to adopt, and had known no major illness for at least half a century. We never thought he would go away just like that, without warning, without a goodbye to his family or without giving his wife and children the chance to tell him how much they loved him.

My sister, his youngest born, the little girl who came along unexpectedly many years after he thought his family was complete, was his favourite child and she returned his love with the same intensity. And so, when he went away abruptly, she was inconsolable. In the days following his passing we worried about her as she withdrew from the world. 'I wish we had told him he had a terminal disease. At least we could have said goodbye instead of just pretending that it would be alright,' she says even today.

For years, Amma's propensity to hold on to all things old, tattered and forgotten got my goat like nothing else would. The tidying-up monster in me saw red every time I came upon some carrybag thrust under her bed, bursting with mysterious, yellow-with-age scraps of paper with illegible scrawls in Malayalam, a tired postcard from the 1970s that had arrived from her home town, dog-eared but tucked away like a precious treasure into the inner pocket of a jaded hand-me-down bag from one of her three daughters.

Saying goodbye is hard, not just to people but to memories and to the things that we associate with those who've left.

When my parents had to leave the ground-floor apartment in the government housing complex they had lived in for thirty years, it was the lemon tree in their garden that Amma missed the most. She had planted it a few years into their stay in that apartment, and some of her happiest memories were associated with that tree. Amma and her aunt, who lived with us until she passed away at the age of eighty-four, tended to the tree as if it were their child, and it returned their love in the form of plump, juicy fruit with which the duo used to make tart, spicy lemon pickle, to be stored in *bharni*s and relished throughout the year. When her kids grew up and left the home and her aunt passed away, it was the lemon tree that helped Amma keep her sanity and rediscover herself. One day, unable to fathom her grief about her now-silent home, we suggested she keep herself busy doing something that she loved. Such as preparing her signature dishes and starting her own lunch delivery service.

'Can I make pickles and lemonade instead?' she asked, her eyes shining at the prospect of finally having something to do that would be appreciated. The first few bottles of lemon pickle and lemonade flew off her kitchen shelf within a day of the announcement of Amma's maiden venture, and she was overwhelmed because it was the first time she was earning any money for her labour. Amma's business picked up rapidly and her depression disappeared magically in between squeezing lemon juice, preparing sugary syrup, sealing and labelling jars of lemon pickle that had to go out to customers, who had stopped making pickle at home because Amma's was better.

Saying goodbye is hard at every stage in life. When I was a teenager there was a boy I knew with whom I thought I was in love. We lived far away from each other, and back in the early 1980s the only way we could communicate was via letters that took painfully long to arrive. I would wait for the letter anxiously all week, and just as soon as the postman arrived, I would grab the mail and retreat to the family's only bedroom where I would sit by the window and devour every word of the letter. They were no romantic letters; just boyish accounts of his days in college, his dreams of pursuing higher education in the US, but I searched and found deeper meaning in every word he wrote. Silly girl that I was, I thought his dreams were our dreams.

My dreams of a journey with that boy proved to be just that but his letters, dozens of them, remained my cherished possession for years, even after I found my life partner and set up our own nest. Years later I came upon the bundle of letters tucked away in a suitcase full of old photographs and letters from dear, departed family members and I still remember the intensity of the pain when I tore up those letters – yellowing with age, the ink fading – into tiny pieces and put them in the trash can. It was as if someone had put a giant hook inside me that was ripping my heart out of my body.

Goodbyes are hard, even if it is to something as simple as sacks full of recipes. At twenty-one, I thought the way to keep my man's love was by cooking him endless varieties of dishes. The recipes remained tucked in a corner cupboard in the kitchen, torn out from different magazines, and put in a folder for me to use someday. I never did manage to make a single dish from the pile of recipes because I got busy with our child, my career, and all the other things that life brought on. One hot summer afternoon, in a paroxysm of intense self-loathing because I was so sad about not being like the other women I knew who cooked dazzling dishes and baked fancy cakes, I sat on the kitchen floor and systematically tore up every one of the recipes. It broke my heart, but I did it anyway and, miraculously, I felt like a caged bird that had been set free.

I know that sometime soon I will have to say goodbye to my little girl who is now a young woman, taller than me and wiser beyond her years. I know she will find a man she loves and set up a home of her own, and I will see lesser and lesser of her.

I hope I would have prepared myself by then to say goodbye with a smile and a hug. I hope I am able to let her fly away happily so she can find her place in the universe. Saying goodbye is hard but I know when we say goodbye at the right time it is one of the most liberating things you can do, because it allows you to walk on this earth with a light and happy heart.

AUTHOR'S NOTE

THIS BOOK IS DEDICATED to my trio of grand-aunts, as feisty a gang of girls as you will ever find, who lived by themselves in a rambling old house on the coast and weathered many a storm in their lives by simply sticking together. They never needed no men and if they ever did, they never did anything conventional about it, such as get married.

This book is also dedicated to my mother who, at seventy, has decided that she will paint her nails every week and exterminate any hair that ever dares to sprout on her chin.

When I was fifteen, I used to think anyone over the age of thirty was old but when I got to that age, tired, a little bruised from giving birth, raising the offspring and the dozen other things I was doing around that time, I discovered being thirty was magical. Thirty was not old. In fact, I was brimming with energy, raring to make the most of my career and the scores of new plans buzzing in my head.

I don't know where the next decade went but when I reached forty, the spring in my step was less bouncy. There were whites on my temples and deep grooves running down the sides of my nose and down to my mouth, grooves that carried my tears – there were plenty in that decade – from my eyes to my chin, from where they splashed onto my laptop because even in those days I was writing away like my life depended on it.

I wrote through everything that happened in my frantic forties – through the first signs of menopause, the soul-searing pain of having my only child go away to pursue her studies, an empty nest, through the numbing reality of seeing my parents ageing and shrivelling up into miniature versions of themselves. I wrote through my bewilderment at my body becoming a stranger to myself and the fact that I was turning into a person whom I would not befriend, if given a choice. I'm talking, of course, of the dreaded hot flushes and mood swings that left me in pools of sweat and great deluges of tears, several times a day.

I wrote away frantically until one day, miraculously, my writing took me past the darkness and I could see the brighter side of my life. At fifty, the very things that scared me about ageing, such as the lines on my forehead and the grooves around my mouth – turned into symbols of a life well lived. The lines around my mouth and my eyes were from laughing out loud and from smiling at the world, and if my hands and legs did not always look well-kept, it was because I worked hard at making an honest living for myself. The faster I wrote and the deeper I went into my writing, the more I was able to see the positive side of my journey until one day, it all started coming out in a series of humorous articles about the bits and parts that make up the life of a fifty-something woman. Some of these appeared in a column I wrote for *Pune365*, a wonderful online community space created by my friend Jaisurya Das. The rest just poured out of me when my kid sister, a spunky, smart woman of the world, told me she loved reading the columns and that I should write a book about the humor of being on the wrong side of fifty.

I have laughed while writing this book and wept copiously too as I wrote about love, loss, parenting, parting, rediscovering myself and finding liberation from my inner demons and the boxes in which I have tried to fit from time to time. I hope that each of you will find something in its pages that touches your heart and makes you laugh. I know some of you might not agree with the way I have looked at my own life or how I have written about it. I have this to say to everyone who reads my book: it has been written from a place of absolute and complete authenticity with no intention to ever hurt or offend anybody. I have simply written about my life and my world the way I have experienced it. And if any one of you would like to share your stories on this subject with me, I am always willing to listen and cheer you along your journey.

This book would never have been written but for the constant encouragement and support of my wonderful family – my husband, my daughter, Amma, my sisters, their loving spouses and my nephews and nieces. To them and to my friends who will find themselves in this book in bits and parts, I have this to say: my life would not be so much fun and such a joyous journey without your presence in it. Amma says my life sometimes looks like a travelling circus and I always tell her to hop on and enjoy the ride. You are all welcome too!

ACKNOWLEDGEMENTS

I WOULD LIKE TO thank my fabulous agent, Kanishka Gupta, who I nagged to death to get this book to a publisher who would believe in it. I am so glad he found Teesta Guha Sarkar at Pan Macmillan India who instantly loved my manuscript and adopted it. I believe some people are meant to be in your life: soon after she started editing my manuscript, Teesta went away from Pan Macmillan for a few months but miraculously came back to the organization less than two months before the book was supposed to go to press! Thanks so very much for taking this book under your wing again and for sharing my excitement about it, Teesta.

I would like to thank my dear friend, Jaisurya Das, for generously allowing me to use some of the columns I had written for Pune365.com, the wonderful online community he has created. I pitched the idea of a 'feisty at fifty' series to him months before I turned fifty and he said yes in a heartbeat. Thank you, Jai – I appreciate the support.

I would like to thank my sister, Sangeeta Menon, who eats books for breakfast, lunch and dinner, for her keen observations about the chapters and for editing them with much love. But for her encouragement, I would never have got down to writing this book. Thanks, Sangi, my book is richer from the love you have showered on it.

And last but not least, thanks to my darling family and friends for providing me wonderful fodder for this book. Writing this book was like a walk in the park, thanks to your presence in my life.